Active Trusteeship for a Changing Era

Gary Frank Petty, *Editor*

NEW DIRECTIONS FOR COMMUNITY COLLEGES

ARTHUR M. COHEN, *Editor-in-Chief*
FLORENCE B. BRAWER, *Associate Editor*

Number 51, September 1985

Paperback sourcebooks in
The Jossey-Bass Higher Education Series

Jossey-Bass Inc., Publishers
San Francisco • London

EDUCATIONAL RESOURCES INFORMATION CENTER

ERIC Clearinghouse For Junior Colleges

UNIVERSITY OF CALIFORNIA, LOS ANGELES

Gary Frank Petty (Ed.).
Active Trusteeship for a Changing Era.
New Directions for Community Colleges, no. 51.
Volume XIII, number 3.
San Francisco: Jossey-Bass, 1985.

New Directions for Community Colleges
Arthur M. Cohen, *Editor-in-Chief*; Florence B. Brawer, *Associate Editor*

New Directions for Community Colleges (publication number USPS 121-710) is
published quarterly by Jossey-Bass Inc., Publishers, San Francisco, CA 94104, in
association with the ERIC Clearinghouse for Junior Colleges. *New Directions* is
numbered sequentially—please order extra copies by sequential number. The
volume and issue numbers above are included for the convenience of libraries.
Second class postage rates paid at San Francisco, California, and at additional
mailing offices.

The material in this publication was prepared pursuant to a contract with the
National Institute of Education, U.S. Department of Education. Contractors
undertaking such projects under government sponsorship are encouraged to express
freely their judgment in professional and technical matters. Prior to publication,
the manuscript was submitted to the Center for the Study of Community Colleges
for critical review and determination of professional competence. This publication
has met such standards. Points of view or opinions, however, do not necessarily
represent the official view or opinions of the Center for the Study of Community
Colleges or the National Institute of Education.

Correspondence:
Subscriptions, single-issue orders, change of address notices, undelivered copies, and
other correspondence should be sent to Subscriptions, Jossey-Bass Inc., Publishers,
433 California Street, San Francisco, California 94104.

Editorial correspondence should be sent to the Editor-in-Chief, Arthur M. Cohen, at
the ERIC Clearinghouse for Junior Colleges, University of California, Los Angeles,
California 900024.

Library of Congress Catalog Card Number 85-60826

International Standard Serial Number ISSN 0194-3081

International Standard Book Number ISBN 87589-741-X

Cover art by WILLI BAUM

Manufactured in the United States of America

This publication was prepared with funding from the National Institute of
Education, U.S. Department of Education, under contract no. 400-83-0030.
The opinions expressed in the report do not necessarily reflect the positions
or policies of NIE or the Department.

Ordering Information

The paperback sourcebooks listed below are published quarterly and can be ordered either by subscription or single-copy.

Subscriptions cost $40.00 per year for institutions, agencies, and libraries. Individuals can subscribe at the special rate of $30.00 per year *if payment is by personal check*. (Note that the full rate of $40.00 applies if payment is by institutional check, even if the subscription is designated for an individual.) Standing orders are accepted.

Single copies are available at $9.95 when payment accompanies order, and *all single-copy orders under $25.00 must include payment*. (California, New Jersey, New York, and Washington, D.C., residents please include appropriate sales tax.) For billed orders, cost per copy is $9.95 plus postage and handling. (Prices subject to change without notice.)

Bulk orders (ten or more copies) of any individual sourcebook are available at the following discounted prices: 10-49 copies, $8.95 each; 50-100 copies, $7.96 each; over 100 copies, *inquire*. Sales tax and postage and handling charges apply as for single copy orders.

To ensure correct and prompt delivery, all orders must give either the *name of an individual* or an *official purchase order number*. Please submit your order as follows:

Subscriptions: specify series and year subscription is to begin.
Single Copies: specify sourcebook code (such as, CC1) and first two words of title.

Mail orders for United States and Possessions, Latin America, Canada, Japan, Australia, and New Zealand to:
Jossey-Bass Inc., Publishers
433 California Street
San Francisco, California 94104

Mail orders for all other parts of the world to:
Jossey-Bass Limited
28 Banner Street
London EC1Y 8QE

New Directions for Community Colleges Series
Arthur M. Cohen, *Editor-in-Chief*
Florence B. Brawer, *Associate Editor*

Contents

Editor's Notes

Over twenty years ago when many community colleges were founded, boards were primarily comprised of professional, business, and civic representatives of the community. These were men and women who brought leadership experience and vision to the creation of board policies. Such boards were inclined to hire presidents who were accustomed to a free hand in carrying out board mandates. Indeed, the respect and personal standing that founding trustees and their presidents brought to their roles gave them credibility and assured otherwise dubious taxpayers and legislators recruited to support the new institutions. For these founders, trusteeship was an important but essentially peripheral part of their lives, most finding fulfillment and recognition in their careers. Political stability, mutual respect, strong presidential support, and longevity of service was characteristic for these trustees and presidents.

Today many, perhaps a majority of, community college boards maintain this long-standing tradition of public respect and community service. They usually do so under more economic and legislative restraints than those of their predecessors. Increasing numbers of minorities and women are especially central to new leadership coalitions; this is very often a parallel to the political power reorganization taking place in communities. Many such boards, typically more representative of their communities, work well and fairly together and with their CEOs. By and large, these boards receive ordinary media attention and very little notoriety. However, some community college boards today are different both in perspective and expectations.

The increased diversity among board members with often dissimilar values and competing priorities has tended to preoccupy the attention of college constituencies and, in some communities, make trustee service itself controversial. Community college trustees, on the whole, are more broadly and intensely active now than in past years as their prerogatives of office have enlarged beyond statutory limits and institutional custom. Learning how to manage their conflicts cooperatively with fellow trustees is a concern of many board members. Past assumptions about board members' relations and roles may need rethinking as trustee involvement gains scope and impact. As a result, attracting and keeping quality trustees has emerged as a prime issue in a growing number of community college districts.

There is a new breed of community college trustee. While the styles and agendas of these trustees are familiar, their cumulative impact has altered the style and substance of board life. These trustees can be helpful in focusing attention on issues not previously addressed by the board, but they may lack an overview and tend to be preoccupied with their own priorities. At least six conduct patterns of such trustees can be identified:

The Presidential Usurper. The role of board member is viewed as one of administrative intervener, sometimes also as confessor for college employees disenchanted with the administration. This trustee may also perform, ad hoc, gratuitous administrative service as needed. Not at all shy, such a trustee may actually establish an office on campus, hire a secretary, issue press releases, and otherwise assume the role of leader in residence, effectively supplanting the president at times.

The Partisan Aspirant. Historically, trustees have not necessarily viewed themselves as perennial candidates for political office. But this member views the trusteeship as a step on the political career ladder or, in some cases, as an interim consolation prize until elected to the legislature or other public office. The college may serve as a showcase for this ambition.

The Special Interest or Adversarial Intercessor. This trustee postures as a friend of the teachers, the union, a taxpayers' association or other groups whose special interest may, in fact, be in opposition to other college constituencies. Such a trustee may also foment adversarial relations between the faculty and administration or other groups. The will of the befriended group may take precedence over the overall interest of the college.

The Crusader or Ideologue. This member brings the passion of a single cause to the board table. The cause may be to stamp out illiteracy, build championship sports teams, ensure institutional commitment to affirmative action, cut college spending on frills, and so on. All college affairs are viewed through the narrow focus of this ideology.

The Vocationalist. For this board member, the trusteeship is a lifestyle, a primary focus, and the principal source of personal recognition and reward. Individual identity, self-worth, even life's meaning (or so it may sometimes seem) are complexly interwoven in the actions and activities of this type of trustee. This trustee, so personally involved in the role as to lose objectivity, requires perpetual "maintenance" by college personnel who are expected to be on call to provide service and attention.

The Terminator. This trustee is out to get someone (often the president) in an effort to vindicate some perceived wrong. Conducted in the manner of guerrilla warfare, the campaign of termination features harrassment, disapproval, rancor, and personal attacks on the subject. The success rate for this type of trustee has been very high in recent years.

These types of trustees may occasionally be found even on boards that function competently and in reasonable coexistence with their presidents. Extreme examples of these types of conduct, however, usually guarantee rancor among board members, withdrawal of good trustees, presidential turnover, or adverse public relations for the college. Inappropriate behavior of this kind may sometimes seem more common among new board members. Some simply have not had previous experience on governing boards or other leadership positions and have no models to emulate. Others may initially respond to the experience of power with behavior that approaches exhibitionism. Over a period of time, some trustees restrict or abandon negative role behavior as maturity or hostile feedback become more manifest. Even with experience, some merely get worse and alienation becomes their norm.

However, the vast majority of trustees are more than willing to learn and grow. A transformation towards responsible behavior can be aided by a planned orientation process of trustee development. It is in the best interest of all involved in community college leadership to promote statesmanlike attributes and conduct among board members. What remains of local control as a governance doctrine and the survival of colleges themselves may depend on such development. Otherwise, state legislators will accelerate what is already a regrettable reality: erosion of local board autonomy through statutory centralization of authority and operational rule making at the state level. Therefore, quality trustees are ultimately responsible for the survival of lay governing boards in postsecondary education.

This volume is offered as a contribution to developing better trustees and represents a variety of viewpoints on the nature and extent of trustee service for this decade and beyond. The sourcebook addresses several areas of trustee involvement from the vantage points of persons whose work brings them in direct contact with the inner workings of boards. Several issues are featured: a demographic and attitudinal survey of trustees in one state, an analysis of the roles of minorities and women as board members, and the function of state and national trustee associations in trustee development. The authors also discuss the importance of trustee participation in collective bargaining, accreditation, public relations, personnel, political advocacy, presidential relations, and board chairmanship. These chapters focus on the strengths and limitations of trustee contributions in key areas of college life. Desirable recommendations for proper board conduct and decorum are included.

It is hoped that these contributions will broaden the field of vision and heighten the compassion and sensitivity of those citizens vested with a public trust worthy of the title trustee.

Gary Frank Petty
Editor

Gary Frank Petty is executive director of the Illinois Community College Trustees Association.

What are the characteristics of community college trustees?
This introductory chapter details the findings of a survey
conducted to provide a demographic and political profile of
the trustees representing the thirty-nine community college
districts of Illinois.

The Illinois Public Community College Board Members

Gary Frank Petty
William E. Piland

Because governing boards are public corporations, they are legally responsible for all college affairs. Yet little is known about the trustees themselves. In fact, a search of the entire ERIC data base yields only three state or national surveys that have been designed to provide information on trustee characteristics (Grafe, 1976; Harkins and others, 1978; Parker and Parker, 1979).

Due to this dearth of information, the Illinois Community College Trustee Association (ICCTA) and Illinois State University conducted a survey in 1983 that provides a useful glimpse into the backgrounds, values, and viewpoints that public community college trustees in Illinois bring to institutional governing boards. The study explored three general areas including trustees' backgrounds (for instance, personal, educational, vocational, and political interests) in addition to their perceptions of trusteeship, their evaluations of the role and effectiveness of their state trustees association, and certain educational issues as viewed by members of the association. The survey polled responses from some 54 percent (141 trustees) of the elected trustees serving the public community colleges of Illinois. Trustees from thirty-four of thirty-

G. F. Petty (Ed.). *Active Trusteeship for a Changing Era.* New Directions for
Community Colleges, no. 51. San Francisco: Jossey-Bass, September 1985.

5

nine community college districts returned survey instruments. The boards of the Chicago City Colleges (appointed by Chicago's mayor) and State Community College of East Saint Louis (appointed by the governor), each with significant minority representation, were not included in the study. In an effort to make the study as current as possible, the same survey instrument was sent to thirty-six newly elected trustees following the November 1983 elections. The percentage of responses (50 percent) and the results were consistent with the data collected earlier from incumbent trustees.

The purpose of this chapter is to present an overview of the study's findings and to briefly discuss what impact trustees' characteristics and viewpoints might have on their activities in the immediate years ahead. Although the study results show trustees' seats dominated by politically conservative, middle, and upper-middle class white males, the trend over the past ten years is toward trustees who are female, minority, more politically aggressive and middle-of-the-road, more visible, to some extent more controversial, and more diverse in socioeconomic outlook. In general, their collective influence through a state association and their perceptions of educational issues may be described as progressive, moderate, and responsive to the needs of communities they serve.

Demographic Characteristics and Educational Background

From those responding, the survey showed that 97 percent of the trustees are white; 76 percent are males, and more than half serve in business-managerial-professional occupations. (Although not reported in the study, it should be noted that the number of female trustees has doubled in the past ten years at the same time that the number of female community college presidents in Illinois has declined by 50 percent, from two to one out of fifty-two campuses.) On the average, a trustee is forty-seven years old, with an income that is either in the $30,000 to $40,000 range (28 percent) or between $45,000 to $60,000 (23 percent). Nearly three quarters of the trustees responding have baccalaureate degrees and more than half have done graduate work at the masters level. About 20 percent of those participating in graduate studies completed doctoral degrees.

Educators represent the largest growing vocational group serving as trustees. The study showed that nearly 50 percent of those responding are employed in education. Twenty-six of the trustees work at elementary or junior high schools, twenty-three work at the secondary level and nineteen are at the four-year college level. Some 15 percent of trustees surveyed had been previously employed at a community college. Among the most recently elected trustees are a former college president, and ex-college vice-president and a former part-time instructor, each now serving on boards that previously employed them. The increasing numbers of educators seeking board seats parallels the rise in the number of educators being elected to the Illinois General Assembly.

Most of the trustees responding (85 percent) have never been employed in a community college, but, of those who had, 12 percent had worked previously at the community college they represent. Only nine percent of the trustees had immediate family members working at the community colleges operated under their boards. A slight majority, 53 percent, had attended a community college while 88 percent of the trustees had some immediate family member who previously or presently attended the community college governed by his or her board.

Political Affiliations and Aspirations

Trustees surveyed are predominantly affiliated with the Republican party (45 percent); 23 percent of the Republican trustees categorized themselves as moderately supportive of the party and 22 percent said they are strongly supportive of the GOP. About 23 percent of the respondents identified themselves as Democrats, but only 7 percent said they strongly supported the policies of that party. With regard to political ideology, the trustees were nearly evenly split between moderate (36 percent) and conservative (33 percent) stances. At the extreme ends, there were only two percent who were strongly liberal and only 14 percent who were strongly conservative. The party affiliation of trustees stands in contrast to the current party line make-up of the Illinois General Assembly. While Illinois has had the same Republican governor for nine years, the Democratic party enjoys override power in the Senate by a thirty-three to twenty-six margin and in the House by a seventy to forty-eight margin. The Democrat majorities, which have grown within the last two statewide elections, may be expected to grow even further during the remainder of the decade. The political implications of this party affiliation contrast between trustees and legislators may increase in importance if more trustees were to address their elections and activities along partisan lines. This does not appear to be a general trend, however, in Illinois.

Is political ambition on the rise among trustees? It would appear from the study that some trustees see board service as a stepping stone to other political offices. There are at least four trustees who aspire to be governor some day, seven who are eyeing a U.S. Senate seat, five who want to be a U.S. Representative, and four who want a state or federal judgeship. Beyond that, sixteen indicated they wanted to be a state legislator, eleven said they sought a city council seat, and eight wanted to be mayor in their communities. One can argue that the trustee as political aspirant can often, through legislative contacts and party influence, help shape the college's fortunes by making it more visible and valuable as a constituent center for politicians. This level of trustee activity accrues real and intangible benefits to the college.

Regardless of political inclination, attracting and keeping good trustees may be a special challenge for community colleges in the future. Of those surveyed, eighty-three trustees said they were encouraged to run by friends, while fifty-one said they were encouraged by other college board members. Another forty-two simply made the decision on their own. Partisan slate-making did not appear to be a factor in most trustee election campaigns. Of those seeking election, 71 percent did so as individuals while only 19 percent ran on informal slates and 10 percent on formal slates with others. Of those who ran with others, in thirty-one cases all candidates on the slate won, while in eleven cases some won and some lost. When asked whether or not they would seek reelection, 71 percent of those surveyed said they would. With respect to campaigning, 23 percent said they had received endorsement from all or most of the media, 16 percent said they had received some endorsement, 40 percent said that their opponents received endorsement, and 47 percent said that the media did not endorse anyone. Though many trustees identified themselves with a political party, 82 percent did not get a party endorsement, compared with 18 percent who did.

One of the most impressive and surprising findings of the study was that trustees on the average had lived in their own community college district for twenty-nine years — most of their adult lives. Also, trustees surveyed had served on the average of six and a half years on the board. Yet even with long board tenure as a norm, it should be noted that in 1983 the State of Illinois mandated six year terms for community college trustees. Previous terms were for four years. More than half of the sixteen incumbent board members who chose not to run in 1983 elections cited the six year term as the reason. Of the estimated eighty-eight trustees scheduled to run for reelection in 1985, it is believed that approximately fifteen to twenty will not seek further service on their boards and that the six year term will be a primary factor in their decision.

Trustee Perceptions of the ICCTA

Another important dimension of this survey was to determine the perceptions the trustees have about their state association. In general, the ICCTA was given a very favorable assessment. Of those surveyed, just over three-quarters said they felt the association was either good or excellent. About seven percent indicated they had no opinion or felt it was poor. The trustees surveyed indicated they valued the ICCTA's new trustee orientation seminar, the trustee professional development programs, major media liaison, and the annual convention.

As far as the legislative functions of the association, the trustees ranked them as follows: monitoring state legislation was first, influencing the state legislature to pass bills favorable to community colleges was second, and liaison with the executive branch was third. It should be noted that political advocacy in the Illinois General Assembly, trustee education, and public relations on behalf of the system are, in order of priority, the three main purposes of ICCTA.

There were a number of functions that the respondents listed as very crucial to the association's operation. The first one was that the ICCTA should monitor federal legislation affecting Illinois community colleges, a role that the association has expanded in recent years. The second was conducting press conferences on important issues affecting community colleges. The third was conducting board/president clinics, and the fourth was developing a code of ethics for boards and presidents. Other important services identified by the respondents included issues clarification, visits by staff, telephone and personal consultations, and assistance with board self-evaluations. The respondents felt the association should have very little to do with issues related to faculty evaluation, course or program development, and board meetings themselves.

The Board/President Relationship

Between July 1982 and March 1985, some nineteen out of thirty-nine community college districts in Illinois experienced a change in chief administrative officer. This is a 50 percent turnover within a four-year period. If campus presidents were included in the figures, the turnover rate would be slightly greater than 50 percent. It is estimated that eleven out of the nineteen chief executives were asked to resign or retire or otherwise found conditions unacceptable for continued employment. The other eight left through normal transitions, such as planned retirement and job advancement. At least six of the firings generated controversial publicity in their respective communities and a few excited commentary throughout Illinois.

A close look at the data behind the dismissals reveals an apparent explanation. It may be that time and circumstances caught up with many presidents as boards themselves changed. Eight of the nineteen presidents who left averaged nearly thirteen and a half years of service in their respective jobs, while the average years of service for all nineteen was nine and a half in a range of four to twenty years. Although 1982–1985 may have been unusual years for presidential longevity, the dramatic turnover has heightened sensitivities and may have raised potentially lasting effects on board/president relations in a state long recognized as attractive to community college leaders throughout the country.

Our survey disclosed board/president relations as a high priority for the association. As a practical matter, however, assistance with board/president relationships as an association service clearly does not mean helping boards resolve disputes with presidents. During the four year period, the ICCTA has, on only one occasion, formally intervened on request to assist in a board/president problem. Most service has been limited to providing general information on presidential searches and conducting workshops on board/president matters. What trustees seem to expect from their state association are aspirational guidelines that local boards may or may not embrace as policy. This expectation is underscored by the fact that only four out of thirty-nine districts have adopted as policy the board/president Code of Ethics that was developed over a two year period between the association and the Illinois Council of Public Community College Presidents. The bottom line is that the doctrine of local board control has its strongest expression in questions of presidential employment.

Linkages with the Community and with Legislators

Another aspect of the survey dealt with trustee/community linkages. We wanted to obtain information about the type and extent of communications the trustees have with the citizens they serve. As to how well the general public was informed about board activities, 11 percent of trustees said they (the general public) were highly informed; 26 percent, reasonably informed; 51 percent, somewhat informed; and 12 percent, not informed. Respondents said they communicated most with college administrators, other board members, and spouses while they had the least communication with college students, state government officials, political party organizations, and citizens' nominating caucuses.

While trustee political activism is on the rise, our experience at ICCTA supports the survey's conclusion that contacts between trustees and legislators may, on some boards at least, tend to be underdeveloped and inconsistent. This fact of trustee life may, for some, reflect a distaste for politicalization of the board member's role, or a feeling that the president should take the lead in legislator cultivation. In any event, this does create special challenges for a state association in building lobbying coalitions in the General Assembly among all 273 trustees, at least a third of whom express no apparent interest in lobbying legislators on behalf of their district or the system. On the other hand, the majority of trustees represent a visible, influential political presence in their communities.

Opinions about Current Educational Issues

The survey asked about perceptions of educational issues in four areas: funding, governance, educational programs, and the statewide system. Trustees overwhelmingly agree that the state should increase funding levels to community colleges, specifically for economic development activity. They disagree that local property tax should be replaced by a local income tax to finance community colleges. In addition, they do not believe that the federal government should provide direct funding for community college operations and that the state variable funding formula should be changed to a flat rate per credit hour.

On the issue of governance, trustees show strong disagreement with a mandatory collective bargaining law for community colleges and strong agreement that boards should retain the option to bargain with a faculty group. Nevertheless, Illinois passed a mandatory bargaining law in 1984, thus further eroding local board control originally authorized when the system was created. Trustees also disagree with these statements: "community colleges are well represented by legislators" "faculty unions work against community college goals," and "the president's role should be one of mediator rather than leader."

In the area of educational programs, only one out of seventeen issues related to educational programs evoked strong sentiment either pro or con: the trustees do not believe that colleges place more emphasis on vocational training than on providing a general education for students. With regard to the Illinois system, trustees do not believe that some colleges should be combined to reduce the number of districts or that some colleges should be closed altogether. There is a strong belief that campus construction should not be financed by student fees.

Finally, what perceived obstacles inhibit boards from achieving goals for their institutions? One hundred and nine trustees said money, fifty-nine said state bureaucracy, thirty-eight said limited physical facilities, thirty-four claimed community apathy, twenty-seven blamed time, and sixteen said faculty.

Implications

We may conclude from the survey that trustees represent a well-educated, financially secure, moderately conservative and increasingly more politically active presence on the boards. Greater diversity in outlooks and background among members may be expected for the remainder of this century. They are, on an average, a very geographically stable cross-section of their respective communities, they devote substantial time to their roles, many work in the field of education, and many have family ties to community college education.

The trustees perceive their state association as an effective group representing their interests in the state capitol, and generally concur on the role, mission, and priorities of ICCTA. A special concern for future boards will be to maintain a stable political climate among members in order to attract and sustain their chief executives.

From the survey, it appears that greater communications by trustees to district communities may need to accelerate as citizen support for tax referenda and local economic development projects through the college become more crucial for institutional survival. More trustees, too, will be expected to activate interest in legislator development. From the state level perspective in Illinois, these changes are already taking place in many districts.

Trustees' strong feelings about maintaining local board control and their balanced views on educational program issues suggest a willingness to lead and an appreciation for educational diversity in the curricula. Trustee concerns about money as the greatest obstacle to achieving goals is borne out by the fact that Illinois state appropriations have declined between 1978 and 1983 from 35 percent to 30 percent of the total operating budgets of districts at the same time that student tuition and local revenue, both with statutory caps, have increased and declined, respectively. The governor's recommended allocation for higher education in fiscal year 1986, however, includes substantial increases in state appropriations for community colleges.

Observable in practice and implied in the results of our survey, the majority of trustees bring to their roles great personal interest and commitment to the success of the colleges they serve. This fact alone ensures positive consequences for trustee activities in the 1980s and beyond, and a bright future for Illinois community colleges.

References

Grafe, G. *The Trustee Profile of 1976*. Washington, D.C.: Association of Community College Trustees, 1976. 20 pp. (ED 128 022)

Harkins, C. L., and others. *A Study of District Governing Boards*. Phoenix: Arizona State Board of Directors for Junior Colleges, 1978. 57 pp. (ED 154 869)

Parker, P., and Parker, P. W. *Decade One + Four: Profile of the Kansas Trustee*. Pittsburg: Kansas State College of Pittsburg, 1979. 27 pp. (ED 181 991)

Gary Frank Petty is executive director of the Illinois Community College Trustee Association.

William E. Piland is associate professor of education at Illinois State University.

The fundamentals of sound board-president relations are
essential to the development of superior community college
boards.

Active Trusteeship for a Changing Era

James B. Tatum

Given the high turnover rate of governing board members and college presidents, it is important to focus on the fundamentals and proven basis of successful trusteeship.

This is especially important in the area of trustee-president relations. Board-president relations are critical to productivity and to the well being of the institution; the more harmonious those relations are, the more the institution will grow and prosper. Though conflict — properly handled — does lead to improved performance, board members should learn to recognize those behaviors that wreak havoc on the attempts of individuals to work together toward common goals. The trustee's first responsibility, then, is to study the fundamentals of good behavior that lead to successful board-president relations.

Evaluating the President

The building blocks of improved board-president behavior are based on the supposition that the board is able to identify its job and to do it. No board member can assess a president with fairness and honesty without knowing what the trustee job is all about. The board, then,

G. F. Petty (Ed.). *Active Trusteeship for a Changing Era.* New Directions for
Community Colleges, no. 51. San Francisco: Jossey-Bass, September 1985.

needs to understand the mission of the institution, embrace that mission, and dedicate itself to seeing that that mission is fulfilled. Mechanisms are further required by which the board can study its role in policy making as well as the president's responsibilities in governance. The board should realize that the president has a very important policy-making role — as a leader, as a consultant, and as a person who makes recommendations. Only through an understanding of these things can the board effectively assess presidential performance.

How is the assessment of this important person to be fairly and professionally accomplished? Presidents frequently complain that they are not being competently evaluated. On the other hand, board members often note that they are not provided with accurate information on which to base the evaluation. Sometimes board members complain that they are provided with too much information. Often different board members will have individual preferences for the amount of information necessary to make decisions. Trustees need to recognize that this circumstance can be very frustrating for presidents because it is extremely difficult to supply information at several levels to suit individual tastes.

These things are necessary in making a professional evaluation of a president:

1. To have a job description and for all parties to know what is really expected of the president.

2. To use annual goals and objectives as a measuring tool for assessment (if this fits the management style) rather than using intuition to make assessments.

3. To require an annual written report from the president to determine whether the board views this report as an accurate statement of where the institution is.

4. To decide what kind of evaluation is to be made; whether it is to be formal or informal, the president must understand where he or she stands and that those personal and processional characteristics will be assessed and jointly discussed.

The level of maturity of the board-president relationship is reflected in the openness of these assessments, both the president's assessment of the board's effectiveness and the board's assessment of the president. The spirit should be one of enhancing growth of the institution through an open exchange of board and president views. It takes a mature group to operate at this level, but it is worth the effort. The defensive nature that sometimes manifests itself in such assessments is nonproductive. It is important to not lose sight of ongoing observations and evaluations made during the year and to learn how to deal with these as they occur rather than to wait for an annual evaluation.

Board Membership and Leadership

Besides presidential assessment, board members need to learn and study a variety of issues: budgeting, goal-setting, strategic planning, and program assessment. Successful trusteeship, then, depends on the skills and competence that board members bring to the task of institutional governance. It follows, then, that the focus should be on the raw materials that go into board membership and leadership. The election or selection of board members is frequently lost in the more glaring issues of conflict of interest, financial disclosure laws, and collective bargaining negotiations. It is small wonder that it is difficult to get the best possible candidates for board members.

One of the most important but least understood areas of college governance is the role of the chairperson in relation to the president and to the board itself. Many systems have been developed to deal with selecting the board chair. Some boards have elected chairpersons almost in perpetuity. Other boards have had rotational procedures, the most extreme being to rotate the board chair every year. In the final analysis, any president will tell you that having a good board chair is critical to good operations. For that reason, it is important for boards to rely on personal qualifications rather than an impartial system in selecting the chairperson. Three personal qualifications should be considered in the selection process: (1) The person should have the time and energy to do the job, (2) the person selected should have persuasive leadership, and (3) that leadership should be the kind of leadership that the rest of the board can embrace. If these ingredients are in place, we can select a person who is the type of public servant and provides the leadership that the board chair necessitates.

Functions of the Board as a Management Team

Given the proper raw materials, boards then need to work as an entity. There must be a mechanism (for instance, board retreats, conferences, and seminars) by which trustees are trained together as a board and brought to a high level of expertise. To create a superior board, we have to elevate the quality and the level of input that goes into the makeup of the board. Quality board-president relations stem from a willingness to become involved and to learn.

The board selects the president; this is the first step toward building a management team. Most presidents cannot survive a poor presidential search, and boards need to know how to conduct the search and what, exactly, they want in a president. Mutual trust and respect are of primary importance to board-president relations, and flaws in the presidential search will retard the growth of a trusting relationship from the start of the president's tenure.

Sometimes the board and the president do not get off to a good start. One of the major problems in board-president relations is the failure to recognize that, when a point of no return has been reached, there must be a separation. It may well be that persons need to leave a board or a president's contract needs to be terminated in order to have a new beginning but, prior to that, there should be a sincere effort to build trust and respect. The importance of knowing what good performance really is and establishing procedures to try to ensure that there is a higher level of performance cannot be overemphasized. It is critical to developing the mutual respect and trust that is so necessary in good college operations. This is not to say that there is agreement on everything but that there must be a healthy respect for the abilities of both the board and the president to listen and come to closure on issues.

This requires us, then, to understand our respective roles. It is one thing to say that the board sets policy and that the president is the chief administrator. However, there are different ways that boards and presidents work together. The board needs to delineate its policy-making role and to identify those items that constitute the role of the administrator. Naturally, there will be variations from institution to institution.

There is a common assumption by trustees that a hands-off approach to the administration is best. However, if we are going to build better institutions, we must take a hard look at the consequences of this attitude. None of us alone has the ability to perform consistently at the same level or to judge ourselves properly, and it is not reasonable to expect this of the president. Checks and balances are necessary to allow the board and president to deal with each other. Furthermore, the board must continue to be informed. The board frequently is the last to know about events that adversely affect the institution. The board and the president must mutually agree on methods of eliminating this unwanted element of surprise.

This does not mean, however, that boards should be overly involved in every facet of administration; delegation is necessary. The board should not act as a rubber stamp. If a board does its homework on recommendations made by the president and if it asks intelligent questions about those recommendations and discusses issues with administrators before ratification, then that is as it should be. But if boards do not do their homework and if boards do not ask questions, then they are acting as rubber stamps.

Unfortunately, board intervention may become necessary because the president has failed in performance or the board has failed to properly delineate the president's responsibilities. Thus, the delegation of power by the board is not absolute. It is entrusted to the president with the proviso that it may be taken back. Board members simply cannot give their power away irretrievably and support the institution on trust.

Thus, there is a need for some tension between the board and the administration. The president and his or her staff need to be studiers, researchers, and analysts who bring recommendations to the board. Trustees, on the other hand, need to be critical in the most positive sense of the word. They need to play the devil's advocate and to keep the administration on a true course. Trustees' questions can perhaps cause administrators to think of things that have not been thought of earlier and to improve administrative responses to institutional problems. No trustee should come to meetings with the attitude that "I will simply be critical." Board criticism needs to come from informed awareness, and it needs to be exercised in the framework of good, responsible behavior.

Conclusion

We as trustees need to renew ourselves in fundamentals, to acutely focus on what it takes to make a good board person and a good board. This chapter has inclined much more heavily towards the side of what is needed from the board member than the responsibilities of the president because that is the author's perspective. Others may take a different approach with the view that the president is all important and that the board means very little. However, many institutional problems testify to the fact that boards have to be dealt with, that the behavior of boards affects institutions, and that understanding the job of being a trustee is very important.

James B. Tatum chairs the Board of Trustees at Crowder College, Neosho, Missouri.

Trustees can play a key role in Congressional lobbying.
Keeping informed of the current legislative scene is vital to
lobbying success.

The Trustee Role in Congressional Lobbying

Sandra L. Ritter

Politics is everybody's business and the fact that decisions affecting education are made in the political arena and will continue to be made there whether or not we become involved, cannot be escaped.

In this vein, it should be noted that government today is even more of a participatory democracy than was envisioned by the founding fathers when they established a government "of the people, by the people and for the people." Constituents are the most important people in a representative's professional life. Members of the House of Representatives depend upon their ability to take the pulse of their districts. In fact, representatives are constantly campaigning. In *The Permanent Campaign* (1980), Blumenthal unravels what he considers "the inside story of the Revolution in American Politics" and reveals "the permanent campaign" as the dominant factor in politics and government today. Brought about by the information age and counterpart of that age, the permanent campaign is the game plan by which a politician can interest his constituents through appearances and rhetoric aimed at the vital concerns of that constituency. Since the majority of a representative's time is spent in Washington while Congress is in session, establishing an information network that enables the representative to gather reliable sentiment to gauge public opinion is necessary. Trustees are becoming a vital

G. F. Petty (Ed.). *Active Trusteeship for a Changing Era*. New Directions for
Community Colleges, no. 51. San Francisco: Jossey-Bass, September 1985.

part of that network and at the same time are making their representatives a part of their educational network.

My dual role as a board member at Oakland Community College and as a district assistant to United States congressman Bob Carr gives me a twofold perspective. It has convinced me that it is definitely feasible to forge effective partnerships between local trustees and their federal representatives. My staff responsibilities include, to a large degree, keeping in touch with constituents and responding to their needs and concerns. We consider their information and help vital to our ability to discharge our legislative duties. As a trustee, I also recognize the necessity of well-researched and accurate facts as well as the added advantage of creating alliances with business, labor, and civic organizations.

Supporting Pro-Education Candidates

A trustee's involvement in the governmental process can take a variety of forms. At the most basic level, exercising the right to vote gives the trustee a chance to select those who will ultimately be responsible for determining the nation's educational policy. Beyond this, active participation in nominating and electing preferred candidates through volunteer activities and campaign contributions adds a tangible sense of commitment to your support. Political campaigns are costly. Monetary contributions are, of course, welcome, but your time and efforts are needed too. By virtue of your place in the community, your involvement is a loud and clear endorsement. Contacting and drawing from the constituents that worked for your own election or appointment demonstrates your willingness to participate in and help develop a network of support for your candidate.

As recent as the 1984 election, faculty unions, community education associations, vocational-occupational associations, and administrative associations identified those candidates that favored education. Incumbents were graded on the basis of their voting records on educational issues and human rights. My congressman received an outstanding report card, and, in turn, qualified for the support of the groups. The educational community became very active in his campaign. Fundraising events, voter information meetings, meet-the-candidate events, and formal endorsements were standard procedure. Individual members walked door-to-door distributing campaign literature, organized neighborhood coffees, and supported Mr. Carr at the polls. Not only was Mr. Carr's information network expanded, but the educational community ensured the election of a pro-education representative in Washington.

Once your candidate is elected, assure him you can be counted on for continued support and information. Become acquainted with the members of his staff. It will be through these people that you will be working to help the member become aware of your concerns and the importance of his support.

Keeping the Congress Informed

How well your information and recommendations are received depends largely on the usefulness, honesty, and reliability of what is presented. Certain measures should be taken before you approach your representative with your special interests. First, review and become familiar with as much material as possible related to bills or issues of importance. This familiarity should include how measures will affect the district beyond that of the educational community. Basically, the knowledge of bill numbers, the status of bills in the legislative process, which organizations are supporting bills, and how the support of targeted measures will conform to the image of the representative projects are essential. By all means, maintain a calm, reasonable, and well-prepared case for your position; be brief and to the point. Refrain from prolonged or controversial arguments, and allow your member to express doubts, questions, and opinions without interruption.

As a staff member, I am able to see how well the system works. In February of 1984, large numbers of vocational-occupational associations converged on Washington at the time when vocational education mark-ups were scheduled. In a concerted, organized effort, association representatives called on key congressmen and provided the information needed to win support for reauthorization. Staff members were invited to lunch where, in an informal setting, the vocational education pitch continued. All these efforts paid off; congress increased vocational education funding and expanded the program to bolster training and retraining for adults as well as the program for technician training assistance within high-tech industries.

Keeping Informed of the Legislative Process

Keeping informed about national legislation is imperative. In planning a lobbying campaign, the trustee should avail him or herself of several other information resources. The ERIC data base is a good place for trustees to start in familiarizing themselves with the federal role in community college education. Examples of pertinent ERIC documents include Davis and others (1983), who detail the history of Title III of the Higher Education Act; Karabel and others (1981), who provide a sociological analysis of federal legislation concerning student aid, community colleges, and postsecondary vocational education; Kim and Wright (1982), who present an evaluation of the Vocational Education Act allocations in California; and Shannon (1984) who discusses the role of federal programs and the mission of the predominantly hispanic community college. The ERIC data base also includes the transcripts of Congressional hearings on educational topics (see, for example, United States Congress, 1981a, 1981b, 1982). Additional hearings and Congressional reports can be accessed through the *CIS/Index*, published monthly by the Congressional Information Service, Inc. Like ERIC, documents indexed in the *CIS/Index* can be obtained on microfiche.

There are a host of other reference tools that can be used to find current information about legislators themselves and about current events in congress. Some of the more prominent are listed below:

1. *Congressional Directory* (Washington, D.C.: Government Printing Office). Issued once every congress, this basic reference tool provides, among other information, short biographies of each senator and congressman, committee listings, and maps of congressional districts.

2. *Congressional Staff Directory* (Mt. Vernon, Va.: Congressional Staff Directory, Ltd.) Published annually, this handbook lists staff members assigned to individual senators and congressmen, as well as the staff who are assigned to senate and congressional committees and subcommittees. Short biographies (including educational and occupational background) are provided for a selection of key staff members.

3. *Congressional Yellow Book* (Washington, D.C.: The Washington Monitor, Inc.) Printed quarterly in looseleaf form, *Yellow Book* provides a directory of congressmen, senators, and their key aides.

4. *Congressional Monitor* (Washington, D.C.: The Washington Monitor, Inc.) Published only while Congress is in session, the *Monitor* provides a daily schedule of upcoming committee hearings.

5. *Congressional Quarterly Weekly Report* (Washington, D.C.: Congressional Quarterly, Inc.) Provides a summary of congressional activity for the current week and follows bills through the legislative process. Of course, it is very important to know who key congressional people are. Tables One, Two, and Three list Congressional committees that deal with educational matters; the tables also identify chairpersons and key aides.

Another important resource is the Association of Community College Trustees (ACCT) and the American Association of Community and Junior Colleges (AACJC). The *ACCT-O-LINE/Federal Focus* is pub-

Table 1. Committees Dealing with Community College Issues:
U.S. House of Representatives

COMMITTEE	CHAIRPERSON	RANKING MINORITY	KEY STAFF MEMBERS
Education and Labor	Rep. Augustus F. Hawkins (D) California	Rep. James M. Jeffords (R) Vermont	Jack F. Jennings (D) Richard D. DiEugenio (R)
Budget	Rep. William H. Gray III (D) Pennsylvania	Rep. Delbert L. Latta (R) Ohio	Richard Q. Praeger Jr. (D) Margaret A. Hostetler (R)
Appropriations	Rep. Jamie L. Whitten (D) Mississippi	Rep. Silvio O. Conte (R) Massachusetts	Frederick G. Mohrman (D) Francis M. Hugo (R)
Science and Technology	Rep. Don Fuqua (D) Florida	Rep. Manuel Luhan Jr. (R) New Mexico	Harold P. Hanson (D) Joyce G. Freiwald (R)

Source: "Key Representatives and House Staff Members in the 99th Congress." *Chronicle of Higher Education*, April 17, 1985, pp. 17–18, 20–21.

lished by the ACCT/AACJC Joint Commission on Federal Legislation and its Director of Federal Relations to keep trustees informed about developing legislation aimed at community colleges. In addition, ACCT actively promotes the involvement of trustees in legislative affairs through its National Legislative Seminar, articles in the *Advisor* and the *Trustee Quarterly*, workshops at ACCT meetings, presentations at state meetings, and direct communication. ACCT's national network of trustees provides a collective voice for making our interests known in Washington. The success of ACCT is based on trustee unity. By staying ahead of federal programs, legislation, and regulations affecting community colleges, we help mold educational policies and programs for the benefit of individual constituencies and for the whole nation.

Conclusion

Though state and local governments have the primary responsibility for setting educational policy and administering educational pro-

Table 2. Subcommittees Dealing with Community College Issues:
U.S. House of Representatives

SUBCOMMITTEES	CHAIRPERSON	RANKING MINORITY	KEY STAFF MEMBERS
Education and Labor— Elementary, Secondary and Vocational Education	Rep. Augustus F. Hawkins (D) California	Rep. William F. Goodling (R) Pennsylvania	John F. Jennings (D) Nancy L. Kober (D) Andrew Hartman (R)
Education and Labor— Post Secondary Education	Rep. William D. Ford (D) Michigan	Rep. E. Thomas Coleman (R) Missouri	Thomas R. Wolanin (D) Marylyn L. McAdam (D) Rose M. Dinapoli (R)
Appropriations— Labor, Health and Human Services and Education	Rep. William H. Natcher (D) Kentucky	Rep. Silvio O. Conte (R) Massachusetts	Frederick Pfluger (D) James M. Kulikowski (R)
Science and Technology— Science, Research and Technology	Rep. Doug Walgren (D) Pennsylvania	Rep. Sherwood L. Boehlert (R) New Jersey	Ezra D. Heitowit (D)

Source: "Key Representatives and House Staff Members in the 99th Congress." *Chronicle of Higher Education*, April 17, 1985, pp. 17–18, 20–21.

grams, presidents and congresses from Jefferson's time have understood that it is in the national interest for the federal government to use its powers and resources to equalize access to education and, through education, improve the quality of American life. The need for federal support of education is clear. Yet, today less than 1.5 percent of the total federal budget is expended on education. Now is the time to become involved.

Looming over us in the 99th Congress is the threat of a restructured federal assistance program for postsecondary students and the consideration of the reauthorization of the Higher Education Act due to expire at the end of fiscal year 1985. Included in the restructuring proposal is the elimination of the Pell Grant Program and State Incentive Grants. A self-help proposal to replace these programs has been

Table 3. Committees and Subcommittees Dealing with
Community College Issues: U.S. Senate

COMMITTEE/ SUBCOMMITTEE	CHAIRPERSON	RANKING MINORITY	KEY STAFF MEMBERS
Appropriations	Sen. Mark O. Hatfield (R) Oregon	Sen. John C. Stennis (D) Mississippi	J. Keith Kennedy (R) Francis J. Sullivan (D)
Appropriations Subcommittee On Labor, Health & Human Services, & Education	Sen. Lowell P. Weicker Jr. (R) Connecticut	Sen. William Proxmire (D) Wisconsin	Marion R. Mayer (D) Rikki P. Sheehan (R)
Budget	Sen. Pete V. Domenici (R) New Mexico	Sen. Lawton D. Chiles (D) Florida	Jan Lilja (R) Janet Holtzblatt (D)
Labor and Human Resources	Sen. Orrin G. Hatch (R) Utah	Sen. Edward M. Kennedy (D) Massachusetts	Kristine A. Iverson (R) David N. Sundwall (R) Mona Sarfaty (D) Dennis F. Hernandez (D)
Labor and Human Resources Subcommittee On Education, Arts, and Humanities	Sen. Robert T. Stafford (R) Vermont	Sen. Claiborne Pell (D) Rhode Island	David W. Evans (D) Polly L. Gault (R) Bruce S. Post (R) Susan E. Franson (R)

Source: "Key Senators and Committee Staff Members in the 99th Congress." *Chronicle of Higher Education*, April 10, 1985, pp. 21–23.

suggested, but it would actually provide 9 percent less money for student assistance. In addition, students would be expected to provide at least $500 (or 40 percent) of their educational expenses, whichever is greater. This will be a significant barrier for poorer students and those who are heads of households. Can your students afford to have a board that is not involved?

Even though congress has made strong attacks on the proposed education cuts, your voice and your involvement in the legislative process is necessary. It is your job to bring education its sufficient recognition. Recognition is necessary of education's complex nature — of its natural entanglement with the economy, of the primary relationship that exists between job skills and education, of the importance of scientific research to our country's continuing as a world leader, of the true value of exposure of diversity of ideas in the sciences and humanities. You are obligated to your constituency to be involved. They have chosen you to be their advocate for education. As elected and governmental appointed officials, you are part of the political world. Do not hesitate to take an active part in the political process.

The community college constituents you represent provide a unique network that is already in place. The college is interwoven with the community it serves. Its linkages with business and industry, its cooperative programs with unions and social service agencies, its advisory groups and its employees represent a broad base that, when assembled, can influence policy decisions. It is time to use these resources and become involved. Lobbying can pay off. Most recently, through collective community college lobbying efforts, the reauthorization of the Vocational Education Act and the Peacetime G.I. Bill were passed. In addition, collective influence succeeded in securing an increase of 25 percent in fiscal year 1985 for student assistance.

Congressmen can be influenced to vote for or against proposed legislation. They are reasonable, concerned individuals who listen to their constituents. They want to know what you think. It's up to you to make your position heard. It's up to you to exert your authority as a spokesman for the people of your community college district. Remember, your constituents are depending on you.

References

Blumenthal, S. *The Permanent Campaign*. Boston: Beacon Press, 1980.

Davis, J.A., and others. *The Anatomy of Institutional Development for Higher Education Institutions Serving Students from Low-Income Backgrounds. Final Report*. Durham, N.C.: Research Triangle Institute, Center for Educational Studies, 1983. 467 pp. (ED 238 322)

Karabel, J., and others. *The Politics of Federal Higher Education Policymaking: 1945-1950. [Report from the] Project on Politics and Inequality in American Higher Education*. Cambridge, Mass.: Huron Institute, 1981. 155 pp. (ED 223 171)

Kim, Y., and Wright, C.E. *An Evaluation of Vocational Education Act Subpart 3 and 4 Allocations in California. 1977-78 and 1978-79*. Menlo Park, Calif.: Educational Evaluation and Research, 1982. 70 pp. (ED 221 704)

Shannon, W.G. "Federal Programs and the Mission of the Predominantly Hispanic Community College." Paper presented at the Hispanic Roundtable Talk of the American Association of Community and Junior Colleges, Phoenix, Arizona, May 23-24, 1984. 16 pp. (ED 244 672)

United States Congress. *Oversight Hearing on Title III of the Institutional Aid Program*.

Hearing Before the Subcommittee on Postsecondary Education of the Committee on Education and Labor. House of Representatives, Ninety-Seventh Congress, First Session. Washington, D.C.: U.S. Congress, House Committee on Education and Labor, 1982. 150 pp. (ED 224 447)

United States Congress. *Oversight Hearing on Tribally Controlled Community College Assistance Act. Hearing Before the Subcommittee on Postsecondary Education of the Committee on Education and Labor. House of Representatives, Ninety-Seventh Congress, First Session.* U.S. Congress, House Committee on Education and Labor, 1981a. 167 pp. (ED 221 238)

United States Congress. *Oversight of Institutional Aid Programs, 1981. Hearing Before the Subcommittee on Education, Arts, and Humanities of the Committee on Labor and Human Resources, United States Senate, Ninety-Seventh Congress, First Session, on Oversight of Title III of the Higher Education Act, Developing Institutions Programs.* Washington, D.C.: U.S. Congress, Senate Subcommittee on Education, Arts and Humanities, 1981b. 109 pp. (ED 217 815)

Sandra L. Ritter is a trustee at Oakland Community College in California.

State legislation has grown increasingly important in two-year college governance. Trustees must take a leading role in organizing the college's lobbying effort.

Trustees as Advocates in State Legislatures

Dan Grady

The increased importance of state legislation in community college governance and education is well documented. Martorana and his colleagues at the Pennsylvania State University have traced the year-by-year growth of state legislation affecting two-year institutions (Martorana and others, 1978; Martorana and Broomall, 1981, 1982; Martorana and Corbett, 1983). Their findings indicate that the amount of state legislation affecting community colleges has increased by 297 percent from 1977 through 1982 (Martorana and Garland, 1984). The state legislature not only decides which of the thousands of proposed and existing programs competing for state funding will receive the financial nod—and to what degree—but it also takes an active role in imposing requirements on community college districts, thus limiting the power of locally-elected trustees.

As competition for state funding intensifies, it becomes increasingly important for community colleges to reevaluate the status of their relationship with the governor's office and state legislature. Implementation of a well-planned program to increase the effectiveness and impact of a district's communications efforts with key legislators is essential and the college trustee can and should play a vital role in this effort.

G. F. Petty (Ed.). *Active Trusteeship for a Changing Era*. New Directions for
Community Colleges, no. 51. San Francisco: Jossey-Bass, September 1985.

An effective communication program should have well-defined short-term goals and employ the most effective implementation method. This could include information dissemination, public relations advocacy, and lobbying. When the goal is to influence legislators, it is essential that everyone involved—especially a member of the board—fully understand the legislative process. A successful lobbying effort can take many forms but the groundwork for this effort should be laid well in advance.

Understand the Legislative Process

To be effective, a trustee must not only have a thorough understanding of the legislative process but also be keenly aware of the names, positions, and committee assignments of key state legislators.

In California's legislature, for example, new legislation must go before a committee—which may have nine to eleven members or more—where a majority vote is required for that legislation to proceed. It is, therefore, important to establish a relationship not only with local representatives but also with every member of committees dealing with education (for instance, policy, finance, budget, as well as the leaders of both parties). Every resource should be utilized to establish such relationships. The record and philosophy of the legislators must be studied and evaluated. Some legislators respond better when approached by faculty, others to students, while some, because of their ambition for higher office, should be approached by the kingmakers of their parties. Too frequently, trustees will overlook the influence of legislative staff members in writing and amending legislation. The staff is often responsible for the final details of legislation after broad policy guidelines have been established by the member. Staff members respond to the same entreaties as committee members.

Those responsible for college lobbying need to do their homework. Gomez (1981) suggests several steps that can be taken to develop a well-prepared lobbying effort:

1. Study the legislative and state budgeting process. It is important to know the committee structure of the state assembly and to know the mechanism of introducing a bill and seeing it through to passage.

2. Before the state legislative session opens, involve college personnel in a one-day workshop to discuss institutional needs and lobbying priorities.

3. Put together a legislative calendar of activities.

4. Foster strong working relationships with local organizations

and groups that can assist the college in getting its message across to the state legislature.

Thus, lobbying begins at the college. A common misconception, as Terry (1982) reminds us, is that the lobbying effort is undertaken at the capital. "The heart of the action mechanism is on campus. Activities at the campus level have an impact on the results at the state capital. But the activities must be planned, organized, and coordinated. . . . All these things must occur on schedule. The legislative timetable is always tight. Failure to adhere to the schedule dooms the program . . ." (p. 85).

Organize the Lobbying Team

There is always a question of who should be doing the lobbying. Should it be the professional educator/administrator? Should it be the trustee? Or should it be a professional lobbyist? Actually, there is an important role for each, and each role is quite distinct. Furthermore, "the task of persuading legislators to nurture community colleges in their policy and financial decisions is an enormous one that cannot be accomplished by the community college trustees alone, or the presidents all by themselves, or the college lobbyists operating by themselves. It is a task that requires true involvement of everyone in the community college system" (Gomez, 1981, p. 8).

Trustees, as elected politicians rather than educators, should know the pulse of the community. They can best approach the legislator because, as elected officials, they are relating on a peer basis, elected official to elected official. Usually, trustees can best address matters of policy, impact on the community, and need for the particular legislation; details are better left to legislative and district staff who deal with day-to-day problems.

The lobbyist's role is slightly different. The professional, paid lobbyist, is on the scene at the Capitol at all times and can more closely monitor the progress of various bills and measures and react quickly. It is essential, however, that the lobbyist be provided with the necessary information from the district and be aware of the district's interests and policies. The professional lobbyist also has the opportunity to work with other professional lobbyists representing various interests and is able to form coalitions and negotiate compromises. He is, or should be, aware of exactly what it will take for a certain piece of legislation to go out of committee or gain those one or two extra votes on the floor that are vital to the legislation's passage. It is also his responsibility to alert the trustees and administration of the college about when they should make a personal visit to the legislature. The lobbyist should also inform them of what needs to be done and whose vote must be switched for a measure to be enacted.

A successful lobbying team should include knowledgeable persons in each of these areas, and all should be skilled and well-prepared.

Involve State Legislators in Local Campus Activities

State legislators are elected politicians who rely on public contact and favorable media exposure to be reelected and continue their public service careers. Thus, a community college board has ample opportunities to help a friendly legislator or to develop new friendships, including: inviting the legislator to visit the district, arranging tours of the campus so the legislator can talk directly to students and know first hand the district's progressive programs and achievements, organizing meetings with key local leaders, or inviting the legislator to address a graduation or dedication of a building. These and other similar activities should be closely coordinated between the district's and the legislator's communications staffs to obtain maximum media coverage of the events.

Assist Elected State Officials with Reelection Efforts

As noted above, state legislators are elected politicians. While community college trustees usually cannot provide the financial campaign contributions that are available from the private sector, the trustee is in a position to influence his own constituents, including his own contributors. As an elected official, the trustee enjoys a certain following in the community and understands the campaign process. If a trustee can demonstrate a significant influence among voters, that trustee will increase his effectiveness with key legislators.

Establish Reputation for Credibility

Developing a reputation for credibility and responsibility is important. It is never too early to develop a positive relationship with those responsible for key decisions that will ultimately affect the local district. Thoroughly identify the individuals who are on key committees, such as education and finance, and familiarize yourself with the governor's staff and that of key state legislators.

The goal of trustees should be to become respected and knowledgeable resource persons so legislators will feel comfortable in contacting them when confronted with matters relating to educational policies on funding. Effective trustees should be recognized as such by legislators and members of their staff alike.

Credibility is earned by consistently providing factual, reliable information. Credibility can also be cultivated in more subtle ways. In governing the local district, the trustee constantly receives a variety of requests or demands. Whenever possible, these should be handled at the local level. The too-common excuse that such requests are out of one's area of responsibility and that the state and the local legislator should be contacted should be avoided. A reply of this type merely passes along the problem to a higher level and causes frustration for the person making the request and for the legislator. Also, it reflects poorly on the trustee and the district. Trustees should take action whenever possible and if it is likely that that action might be appealed, should inform the legislator of the rationale. Being informed, the legislator is less likely to act against the trustee's interest. The legislator will also appreciate being relieved of petty annoyances.

Trustees should demonstrate to the legislator that their every action is well thought out and responsible and should govern the district in a manner that is a credit to the district. Trustees should avoid drawing unfavorable attention to the district. A constant stream of negative press relating to trustees or the college district will diminish district influence with the legislature.

It is important, also, that the trustee develop strong relationships with local business and community leaders and be active in organizations such as the Chamber of Commerce, local community groups, and taxpayers' associations. Through this exposure and participation, credibility and visibility will increase.

Once the trustee has established a solid, credible relationship with key individuals, the task as an advocate for the district will be easier. The trustee will be speaking from a position of strength and legislators will know the trustee's reputation, background, and influence in the community.

Develop an Imaginative Approach

As a trustee, many resources are available. Staff members can furnish facts, figures, and other research information that can be used effectively in presentations. The public information office or the college speakers' bureau are such resources. The trustee should make an effort to know and fully understand staff member's respective responsibilities and capabilities. He or she also should be aware of publications produced by the district and request that the public information officer provide clippings of important news items that have appeared in the local media.

These are trying times for community colleges. As the federal government attempts to lower expenditures and reduce taxes, states are sure to follow in the same path. Furthermore, as every activity and each special interest group — both inside and outside education — competes for a bigger piece of the annual budget pie, it may be that only those implementing the most thorough and creative approaches of advocacy will be efffective in achieving their goals.

References

Gomez, A. S. *Politics in Education: A Case Study of the Florida Community College System Legislative Program with an Emphasis on Miami-Dade Community College Activities.* Miami, Fla.: Miami-Dade Community College, 1981. 38 pp. (ED 212 338)

Martorana, S. V., and Broomall, J. K. *State Legislation Affecting Community and Junior Colleges, 1980.* (Report No. 37.) University Park: Center for the Study of Higher Education, Pennsylvania State University, 1981. 146 pp. (ED 206 337)

Martorana, S. V., and Broomall, J. K. *State Legislation Affecting Community, Junior, and Two-Year Technical Colleges, 1981.* (Report No. 38.) University Park: Center for the Study of Higher Education, Pennsylvania State University, and the National Council of State Directors of Community Junior Colleges, 1982. 182 pp. (ED 219 121)

Martorana, S. V., and Corbett, P. C. *State Legislation Affecting Community, Junior and Two-Year Technical Colleges, 1981.* (Report No. 39.) University Park: Center for the Study of Higher Education, Pennsylvania State University and the National Council of State Directors of Community Junior Colleges, 1983, 223 pp. (ED 231 481).

Martorana, S. V., and Garland, P. H. *Highlights and Overview of Actions of 1983 State Legislative Sessions Affecting Community and Two-Year Technical Colleges: A Report to the National Council of State Directors of Community and Junior Colleges.* University Park: Center for the Study of Higher Education, Pennsylvania State University, 1984. 19 pp. (ED 264 945)

Martorana, S. V., and others. *Dollars and Directives: Issues and Problems Related to Financial Support and Legal Authorizations of Community Colleges.* Washington, D.C.: American Association of Community and Junior Colleges, 1978, 60 pp. (ED 156 295)

Terry, J. N. "Toward Effective State Legislative Relations." In P. Bryant and J. Johnson (Eds.), *Advancing the Two-Year College,* New Directions for Institutional Advancement, no. 15. San Francisco: Jossey-Bass, 1982.

Dan Grady is a trustee at the San Diego Community College District in California.

Community colleges serve large proportions of the minority students in higher education. This chapter, based on a national survey, examines the growing role of minority trustees in the college governance system.

Characteristics of Minority Group Trustees

Jerry Lacey

Community colleges have outgrown the status of simple institutions; many have become large, complex organizations of students, faculty, and administrators who represent a wide range of ideas and backgrounds. Because of its very nature and function, higher education is set apart as a unique social system (Bawler, 1962). One aspect of the organizational structure of education is a lay governance system. Considerable attention has been given to the role of trustees and lay governance in the literature of higher education; however, there is little information in the literature concerning minority trustees' influence and involvement in community college governance.

At the 1984 Association of Governing Boards National Conference on Trusteeships, the experience and concerns of minority board representatives were discussed. John King (1984), a trustee of the College of the Ozarks, distinguished visiting professor at the University of South Carolina, and former president at two universities, stated, "Being a minority trustee on any governing board is a severe test. Serving on a board that is predominantly white or black or otherwise racially preponderant can be more than a minority member with dignity — of any extraction — can tolerate. However, such service need not

G. F. Petty (Ed.). *Active Trusteeship for a Changing Era.* New Directions for Community Colleges, no. 51. San Francisco: Jossey-Bass, September 1985.

be an overwhelming difficulty; I have seen crucible situations develop in some instances, ennoblement in other" (p. 21).

At a time of expanding minority enrollment, it is appropriate that the concerns of minority trustees are properly noted. This chapter reviews the findings of a national survey conducted in late 1984 that recorded such concerns. The survey was targeted to the approximately 400 community college trustees who are ethnic minorities; 113 minority trustees responded. The findings are discussed below.

Survey of Minority Trustees

Personal Characteristics. Males constituted the largest portion of minority trustees (59.2 percent) as compared to (40.7 percent) female respondents. The survey showed that 79 percent of the minority trustees were black, 10.7 percent were hispanic, 3.6 percent were Indian/native American; 4.4 percent were oriental/asian American; and .9 percent were other minorities. Within racial groups the male-female ratio was as follows: blacks, 58.6 percent male and 41.3 percent female; Hispanic, 81.8 percent male and 18.1 percent female; Indian/native American, 50 percent male and 50 percent female; oriental/asian American, 60 percent male and 40 percent female. The majority of the minority trustees were in the age range between forty-one to fifty (32.6 percent) and fifty-one to sixty (30.6 percent).

In the area of occupation, 25.9 percent served as administrators and 18.5 percent (each) were in business/managerial and professional positions. The salaries of over 50 percent of the minority trustees were in two groups: 27.4 percent in the $45,000 to $60,000 range; 23.4 percent in the $15,000 to $30,000 range. However, an additional 21.5 percent were in the $30,000 to $45,000 range, 10 percent were $75,000 and over, and 5 percent were $15,000 or under. Twelve percent had a baccalaureate degree, 13.8 percent had done some graduate work with 42.5 percent having completed a masters degree. As a group, 68.3 percent of the minority trustees had at least a baccalaureate degree.

Minority trustees usually had lived in their community college district for a number of years: 21.3 percent lived in the community college district twenty to thirty years and 47.5 percent for over thirty years. Even though minority trustees lived in their district for long periods of time, they were relatively new to serving on the board: 65.4 percent had served five years or less and a cumulative 84.4 percent had served less than ten years.

Friends (16.7 percent) and political party organizations (14.2

percent) were two groups that provided these minority trustees the most encouragement to run for the board of trustees. "Deciding pretty much on one's own" was the third choice, with 11.8 percent. Nearly three quarters (72.5 percent) of the minority trustees ran for the board as individuals rather than as a part of a formal or informal slate. An overwhelming majority of 82.5 percent said they would seek reelection if they had to make that decision today. Minority trusteees judged the three most important characteristics a community college trustee should have to be: (1) sufficient time for duties, (2) stature in the community, and (3) ability to compromise.

Opinions About Effective Trusteeship. When asked to compare their present board with past boards in their districts, 57.9 percent of the minority trustees felt that the present board was rated as poor in representing the views and opinions of district citizens, and 49 percent felt the present boards were poor in providing leadership for the district. The greatest obstacle that inhibited boards from achieving their goals were considered to be lack of money (57 percent) and state bureaucracy (33 percent). In the area of trustees' activities and trustee effectiveness, 92.7 percent felt that influencing state legislation affecting community colleges was the most important activity and 86.3 percent rated their effectiveness in this as good to excellent. The next most important activity was liaison with the executive branch, as indicated by 91.8 percent of the respondents, with an effectiveness rating of good to excellent given by 85.4 percent of the respondents.

In lay governance, there is a great deal of interest in the factors or groups that exert influence on trustees' decision making. Minority trustees (80 percent) reported that they were influenced most by the president/chancellor. "Other trustees in the district" was the next most influential group, as indicated by 51 percent of minority trustees. However, minority trustees felt that different factors or groups influenced their fellow board members. Ninety-three percent of the minority trustees felt that "college administrators other than the president/chancellor" had the most influence on their board colleagues, and faculty members were perceived to be next most influential group.

Minority trustees identified nine major responsibilities of a board of trustees. At least 80 percent of the responding trustees agreed or strongly agreed with each of these items. The following list identifies these items in descending rank order of agreement (from the 93 percent to the 80 percent).

1. The board should have a concise set of by-laws that provide clear duties for the officers of the board and spell out the procedures by which the board transacts its business.

2. The board members should use their status in the community to bring about better understanding of the college's aims and programs.

3. The board should have an orientation program for new members to familiarize them with board policies and goals.

4. The board should evaluate the chief executive officer annually.

5. Working relations between the chief executive officer and the board should be clearly defined and understood.

6. Board meetings should be characterized by free discussion, general participation, and active thinking.

7. The board should not allow faculty members to have a voice in formulation of district policy.

8. Board meetings should deal primarily with policy formulation, review of plans, making board authorizations, and evaluating the work of the district.

9. The board should not conduct an annual review of its own organization and work.

Regarding the board's authority to release faculty or staff for making statements or engaging in activities that the board interprets as detrimental to the district, approximately 40 percent of minority trustees agreed or strongly agreed, 47.6 percent disagreed or strongly disagreed, and 13 percent were neutral on the role of the board of trustees in this matter.

Another finding of the study was the minority trustees' ranking of the responsibilities of the board members in order of importance. The trustees perceived the responsibilities as

1. Establishing institutional policies,

2. Selecting and terminating, if necessary the chief executive officer,

3. Evaluating the performance of the chief executive officer,

4. Establishing a budget,

5. Fulfilling trustee committee assignment,

6. Serving a public relations function for the college district,

7. Communicating the needs of the district to state officials,

8. Taking personnel actions, including the hiring and firing of administrators and faculty,

9. Determining whether the college district is meeting the needs of community groups, and

10. Deciding on changes in the curriculum.

College Role. Minority trustees felt that vocational/technical programs were the most important part of the two-year college curriculum;

college transfer programs were rated next in order of importance, followed by adult and continuing education. When asked, however, which curricular areas the college wanted to give more emphasis, the respondents indicated the transfer function, followed by vocational/ technical training and retraining programs. Over 75 percent of the minority trustees indicated that the community college should really focus on the following matters:

1. Intensify their efforts to secure private contributions for financing operations.

2. Approach local businesses for funds to finance operations.

3. Increase state funding for economic development activities.

4. Host regular informal discussion sessions for community members.

5. Be as concerned about the personal values of its students as with their intellectual development.

6. Add only new programs for which the local community has demonstrated a proven need.

Minority Trustees: Conclusion. Minority trustees are well-educated, long time residents of their community college districts. They are in administrative, professional, and business/managerial positions; they are knowledgeable about educational issues and are committed to providing quality education to all students in higher education.

References

Bawler, N. W. "Who Should Be in Charge of the Department, Head or Chairman?" *Journal of Higher Education*, 1962, *33*, 315–318.

King, J. "Minority Trustees Face Special Challenges." *Association of Governing Board Reports*, 1984, *26* (5), 20–25.

Jerry Lacey is president of the Illinois Community College Trustee Association and is trustee at John A. Logan Community College in Carterville, Illinois.

Women have found places on boards of directors of many
types of organizations. This chapter reviews their status on
community college governing boards.

Characteristics of Female Trustees

Sheila M. Korhammer

Many of the women elected or appointed to community college governing boards have made significant contributions to the progress of the
institution. However, many of them have had difficulty becoming part of
the board team. Anyone, male or female, who perceives himself or
herself to be an outsider is not going to be a viable contributing decision
maker but will instead be a weak, if not broken, link on the team chain.
Women are more likely than men to feel like outsiders and suffer from
the feeling that they lack a sufficient amount of power and control.
Shared power and control requires that each person has an equal chance
to influence outcomes. The link between outcomes and good working
relationships is indisputable.

A survey administered to the 918 female community college
trustees yielded a 42 percent response. Summary findings of the national
survey of female board members revealed that the average female
trustee was fifty years or older, Caucasian, had served on her board for
six or fewer years, and had done at least some graduate work. She was
employed full-time in business related employment and was a moderate
Democrat. She shared responsibility for the income supporting the
household but did not have the primary home management responsibility for children living in the household. She was very busy in other
community volunteer activities, as indicated by a 92 percent positive
response. An 82 percent negative response indicated that she was most

G. F. Petty (Ed.). *Active Trusteeship for a Changing Era.* New Directions for
Community Colleges, no. 51. San Francisco: Jossey-Bass, September 1985.

likely not an alumnus of her college. She was recruited to serve as a trustee and attended an orientation that was presented by the president or a combination of board and administrators. Her motives for agreeing to serve were, primarily, an interest in education and a desire to provide a valuable community service. She felt valued as a trustee and felt that she contributed to key decision making. She was certain that the other board members would elect or reelect a woman as chairperson within the next five years. She was positive about her board's involvement in its affirmative action plan and was satisfied with her institution's efforts to recruit and employ qualified women and minority applicants.

Beyond the raw data, however, the survey responses revealed great intensity of feelings, especially on the problems faced by women on community college boards. The following sample of comments from women in various states is illustrative:

Stop thinking of women as "sexual groupies." The "NOW" group has stereotyped elected women. We are no better or worse than elected men. We are individuals, and behave as individuals. If you remove the word "women" from your question(naire) it gains validity in my mind. (California)

I have been the only woman trustee since I was first appointed (to replace the first woman ever to serve). . . . My "assertiveness" was developed early in life and has served me well. New male trustees may begin with a patronizing attitude (lots of them), but I don't put up with much of that. (California)

It has taken years to establish my credibility with male colleagues, and I was not elected board chairperson until a second woman was elected to the board and provided the needed vote. It is a continuing struggle to be perceived as other than "a woman member." (California)

We are all trustees—whether we are men or women, black or white, hispanic or other. I'm concerned that being concerned with the student, the school, the community is the prime emphasis of being a trustee. We do not represent women or any other specific group. We are a part of the community. I served as board chairman for two years. I'll probably serve again in the new term. Do not divide—we are there for the same purpose. (Arkansas)

In our rural area, it is generally a "man's world." It is hard for women to be elected as chairman of anything — let alone a college board. Perhaps something may be done to show that women are capable and very devoted to a good cause. (New Jersey)

I don't feel you should even suggest that women are treated differently. If a woman has worthwhile ideas and presents them intelligently, she will be accepted as any board member. She has a job to do and she should do it in the best possible way without hurt feelings. She is not there as a popularity contestant. She is there to help make decisions and that she should do as should every board member. (Arizona)

Quit thinking of people as men or women and consider them as individuals! Don't make a career of either sex or ethnic background! It is what is inside that matters. (Kansas)

We need all the help we can get as we sit alone in a room of men. (Texas)

As can be seen from the above quoted comments, sentiments were diverse. However an analysis of the comments indicated that a majority (57 percent) of the respondents offering comments felt either that women frequently were not treated as equal board members by their male colleagues or that at least some training was needed to help women overcome the obstacles frequently set up by their male fellow board members. Thirty percent of the written comments supported the concept that there was no problem and that too much attention was being given to an arena in which there were no combatants. The remaining 13 percent made general comments or felt that there was an overlap in their feelings as they vacillated between both attitudes, as is demonstrated by a comment from a woman trustee in Florida, "Maybe an orientation [should be held] for new women trustees. Women should be super prepared for board meetings and be politically active. Generally, I feel women should not be given 'special' programs — we all (men and women) are trustees — gender should not be a factor as race should not be — but maybe that is wishful thinking."

Since a board of trustees is a team, resolving these issues is critical. Two factors important to each individual team player are, "Am I in or out?", and, "Do I have any power and control?" Shared power and control in the team means giving each person an equal chance to influence outcomes, but this goal is often not achieved, because many men (and also many women) are not comfortable with women having power. A respondent from Canada wrote, "I was appalled to encounter a woman vice-chair from the northeast region who accepted the fact that her role as vice-chair would not lead to the chair — in fact had been leap-frogged over at least once." It would seem that not only was this woman's board reluctant to move her to a position of power, she herself was resigned to her role. The question could be raised as to this woman's competency to fulfill the responsibilities of the chair, but this scenario is too familiar and suggests that many competent women are expected to be mollified with a token vice-chair appointment. Also, from North Carolina came the request, "Encourage male trustees to give women responsible assignments. I have more business experience than some male trustees, but women will not be considered to serve on the financial committee or to chair a committee."

How can women overcome these barriers? Josefowitz (1983) outlines seven "internal roadblocks of women's socialization" that should be considered:

1. Authority — for most women, this has always been in the hands of others, such as parents and teachers.

2. Assertiveness — as relates to role expectations, assertiveness in men is considered aggressiveness in women.

3. Accountability — women are seen as harmonizers, mediators, fearful of delegating.

4. Accessibility — women are accustomed to meeting the needs of others.

5. Affiliation — women depend on existing friendships, a need to be liked. (Josefowitz goes on to say that boys play for the pleasure of sport, girls play for the pleasure of being together; that girls share intimate thoughts and feelings, boys share experiences.)

6. Approval — it is believed that women are most likely to seek approval rather than constructive criticism, and women tend to consider disapproval personal.

7. Affability — it is expected that women should not muddy the waters or stir up conflict. Instead they should be nice, polite, gentle, calm, mild, and helpful. As a result women have difficulty confronting or criticizing (adapted from pp. 15–18).

The "seven A's" summarize the major areas that hinder the decision-making effectiveness of women. What makes this problem most serious is that these roadblocks are both internal and external, involving women's self-perceptions and their perceptions of others.

It is interesting to note that training program needs for women as communicated by survey respondents mirror the problem areas outlined by Josefowitz. A Michigan respondent asked for "consciousness or awareness raising activities to indicate the leadership potential and contributions of women." The respondent also cited the need to "build self-esteem so that 'group think' and male presidents will not intimidate women to self-censor ideas or proposals. Women are potentially strong change agents for [the] higher education system of America." A respondent from Illinois saw the need for a "seminar for women trustees and women minority trustees to improve communication skills and tactics that would help women trustees to articulate their ideas and positions without their male counterparts labeling them as being emotional or over reacting." Another Illinois respondent observed "that women have to work harder than men to prove their effectiveness. I would suggest a program for male trustees that would facilitate them in accepting women as capable decision makers. This would benefit women."

However, many respondents did not see the need for special assistance. One of the major deterrents to women's success on their boards is their own self-image. Before women can expect men to change their perceptions, women must change their own self perceptions. A woman who does not see herself as an intellectual equal to the men on her board lacks the self-confidence necessary to win that equality. Not all women will have this problem and the ones who do not will probably have difficulty relating to the problems of those women who do. This became apparent from the comments of several women who responded to the questionnaire. From Canada: "Women trustees are not different from males in so far as their role as trustee is concerned, or the kind of job they do in that role. Training that would benefit males would equally benefit females and vice versa." From Florida: "Why are women trustees different?" From Illinois: "Women in the role of trustee must be integrated as part of the 'whole.' Separate activities, workshops, or discussion groups would serve no real purpose. If a woman trustee feels alienated or apart from her board, she should take the initiative to rectify the situation. As a former board chairman, I feel that a woman (as well as a man) is recognized for the contributions she or he makes, not only on community college boards, but in all activities of life." Thirty percent of those making written comments took forceful exception with special programs for women trustees. This definitely could not relate to respondent's expressing the need for specially designed programs for women.

Considering those respondents making written comments in support of special efforts on behalf of women trustees, it is interesting to assess the statistics relating to the self-perceptions of all respondents to

48

the questionnaire (including those not offering written comments). The perception that, as individuals, they had input to and impact on board decision making was overwhelmingly positive. In response to the question, "Is your input valued as much as that of other trustees?", 76 percent said, "yes, often"; 16 percent said, "yes, occasionally," and only 8 percent responded, "no, not often," or "not sure." Similarly, when asked, "Do you feel you are contributing to the key decisions of the board as much as other trustees?", 88 percent responded in the affirmative while only 6 percent said, "no" and 6 percent declared they were not sure.

Nonetheless, the influence of women trustees is increasing. Several have distinguished themselves through major accomplishments on behalf of community colleges at all levels, but particularly at state, national, and international levels. They serve as role models and as the nucleus of an "old girl's" community college network that will help women trustees overcome the problems cited by many of the survey respondents.

Conclusion

In order to meet the challenges of today's society, we must have competent leadership. Women trustees are requesting and expecting to receive their share of the governance responsibility for community colleges. Community colleges need strong and effective management. Also, the traditional academic structure is changing—there are more minority students, more high technology programs, more women students, and fewer resources to support our programs. The future of our country will depend on our ability to work together and meet the educational challenges of today and tomorrow.

Reference

Josefowitz, N. *Paths to Power*. Reading, Mass.: Addison-Wesley, 1980.

Sheila M. Korhammer is a trustee at Northampton County Area Community College in Bethlehem, Pennsylvania, and past president of the Association of Community College Trustees.

Participation in professional organizations, involvement with special interest committees, and attendance at meetings, seminars, and conventions are important trustee obligations.

Trustee Participation in Professional Activities

Wayne T. Newton

As the community college movement has progressed and expanded over the past two decades, the role and responsibility of the local trustee has also changed to reflect that growth. The era is long since past when trustees could devote their time and energy exclusively to the development of their local institutions without thought to state, regional, and national activities. Decisions made at the state and national level exert considerable impact on even the most autonomous, locally-controlled institution. Along with the growth of the community college network has come the necessity for interdependence and cooperation among two-year institutions in order to effectively and efficiently meet the goals set forth. As community college trustees, we have found strength in numbers and have discovered that the influence of 1,219 community, junior, and technical colleges united in effort can literally move mountains in Washington, D.C., and in our individual state capitals. We are a force to be reckoned with, and we continually add to the list of our combined accomplishments in our quest to meet the educational needs of our community's adult learners.

The success we enjoy, however, comes from the hard work and dedication of those local trustees across the country who continue to give their personal time and energy to support the variety of issues impacting

G. F. Petty (Ed.). *Active Trusteeship for a Changing Era*. New Directions for Community Colleges, no. 51. San Francisco: Jossey-Bass, September 1985.

community college governance. Unfortunately, only a percentage of the approximately 7,500 local board members have the interest or the time to devote to professional activities outside of their own institutions. In fact, in the past many local trustees gave little regard to regional or national concerns. This situation is changing, however, as more trustees have an opportunity to attend meetings, serve on committees, and represent their colleges in a variety of national forums.

The profile of the typical community college is changing in keeping with the changes in our institutions and the populations we serve. Board membership in the 1980s requires far more than personal friendships or political favors and involves more time commitment than the few hours per month to attend the local meeting. As a result of their survey of community college trustees in Michigan, Pappas and Ritter (1983) have compiled a profile of respondents. They report that the typical trustee in that state is male, aged fifty-one to sixty, employed or self-employed in a professional occupation, and has served on the board for more than seven years. Although these characteristics have been common among trustees across the country, the trend appears to be changing. More often, newly elected or appointed board members are young professionals who are energetic and enthusiastic about their roles as trustees. Often, these new members are women or minorities. They are more active on their own boards as well as on the national scene. In fact, many more trustees now consider advocacy a responsibility of their position, instead of viewing their role solely as a protector of the local tax dollar or as a way to advance their political careers. As these trustees become more experienced and aware of the issues affecting the future of their own institutions, they will provide additional input, support, and leadership for their state and national associations.

The national Association of Community College Trustees (ACCT) spends a major part of its effort and resources in assisting local district trustees to become aware of and involved in national activities. Membership in ACCT assures the local institution of support and representation at the national level. The function of the organization is to provide a national perspective on issues of concern to its members and an avenue for local participation in national activities.

Among the more notable of the ACCT activities are the eight regional seminars, the national legislative seminar, and the annual convention sponsored by the Association. Attendance at these events has increased dramatically in the past few years. From 153 participants registered for the annual convention in 1970, attendance has grown to 1,500 registrants at the 15th annual convention held in San Antonio, Texas, in the fall of 1984. The annual legislative seminar attracted over

500 participants in February 1985. The eight regional seminars are also popular and have enjoyed record-breaking attendance figures this past year. The growth in attendance can be attributed to several factors, among them the quality of the programs, the currency and urgency of the issues discussed, the excellent reputations of presenters and keynote speakers, and the growing interest of local board members in national concerns. In addition to a wide variety of topics and sessions offered at the annual convention, there is provision made for special interest groups, committees, academies, and assemblies to meet during the convention. The convention program and facilities are designed to make it easy for trustees to become involved and to participate in an area of interest or concern to them and their institution. Not only is it convenient to participate, but each trustee is encouraged to assume an active role in the five-day conference. Board membership takes on a broader perspective after attendance at such a national meeting and the experience follows the trustee back to his or her home institution. Sharing that experience with fellow trustees reinforces the desire to maintain or increase activism at the national level.

Of special interest to a growing number of trustees across the country is the annual national legislative seminar held in February in Washington, D.C. Last year's seminar was an especially interesting and informative session and provided opportunity and encouragement to participants to actively seek out their state representatives and make them aware of the issues of concern to higher education, in particular to community colleges. This was an especially critical meeting in view of the pieces of legislation pending that would directly affect daily operations at the local institution. Trustees with little or no experience in the political arena found themselves actively lobbying for their individual special interests and for collective concerns.

These trustees are not alone in their attempt to influence our legislators and participate in decision making at the national level. The combined forces of the AACJC/ACCT Joint Commission on Federal Relations has proven to be invaluable in educating members of Congress about issues affecting our nation's community, junior, and technical colleges. The Joint Commission, comprised of both trustees and college administrators, is effective at identifying critical issues and initiatives, determining priorities, and developing strategies to support the passage of key legislation. With the unified effort of both community college associations, considerable progress has been made in influencing law makers and creating awareness in the nation's capitol as well as in our own state capitols.

Such national leadership does not evolve without personal desire and effort on the part of the trustee. Although each individual can make a difference and can make his or her voice heard in state and national forums, the trustee must have a thorough understanding of the issues in order to effect necessary change or to participate in the decision-making process.

ACCT will lend support and encouragement for such professional endeavors. It is committed to educating, informing, and assisting trustees in developing their skills of boardmanship. Recognizing that most board members assume their position with little or no knowledge of community college governance and with little preparation for trusteeship, the association makes available a variety of orientation materials and conducts special sessions for new trustees at its annual convention. ACCT executive director William Meardy (1984) makes a case for such trustee education in his statement, "Taxpayers have a right to expect that governing board members obtain the necessary tools of boardmanship in order to best hold in trust the huge business enterprises that community colleges represent. . . . Taxpayers do not believe that trustees can do the best possible job unless trustees belong to organizations that are specifically designed to meet lay educational needs. And, once trustees belong to those organizations, they should actively participate in activities in order to benefit from the programs and services that are offered" (p. 3).

In fact, the Board of Trustees of Muskegon Community College in Michigan has taken this message to heart and has formulated a specific policy addressing trustee education. It reads: "Board members are expected to participate in educational activities that enhance their ability to govern effectively. . . . To support this effort, the College shall maintain membership in state and national educational trustee organizations . . . the chairperson will . . . assure institutional representation, encourage trustee participation, and approve expenses" ("Board Policy on Trustee Education," 1984, p. 3).

The key effectiveness at the local board level is the activism of each trustee. The function of a trustee is to establish policy and set institutional direction and trustees must be aware of the impact of critical issues and decisions made beyond the local college. To be a truly effective advocate for the community college, a trustee should play an active role in influencing and shaping those decisions that affect our organizations at both the state and national level.

Participation in professional organizations, attendance at meetings, seminars, and conventions and involvement with special interest committees, all provide opportunities for trustees to share experiences and ideas with colleagues from across the country and to form alliances that will strengthen the national network. Such activism certainly demands time, energy, and effort, but there are many rewards for those willing to become involved.

References

"Board Policy on Trustee Education," *Association of Community College Trustees Advisor*, January 1984, p. 3.

Pappas, R. J., and Ritter, S. L. "Survey Finds Administrators, Trustees Differ On Roles," *Community and Junior College Journal*, October, 1983, p. 18.

Meardy, W. H. "The Importance of Trustee Education," *Association of Community College Trustees Advisor*, January 1984, p. 3.

Wayne T. Newton is chair of the Board of Directors for Kirkwood Community College, and president of the Association of Community College Trustees.

Trustees have an important role to play in maintaining good college-media relations.

Media and the Trustee

Jan Hamilton
Raymond Hartstein

If you ask any community college trustee what he or she least enjoys about the job the answer is likely to be press relations during a college crisis.

Trustees complain:

"Why does the press always sensationalize news?" "Why do reporters always take things out of context?" "Why do the papers report wrong facts?" News reporters complain: "What are the schools trying to hide?" "Why do the trustees evade our questions?" "Why do we have to wade through 'puff' terminology before we get to the real news?"

Cutlip and Center (1982) note that "organizations want news reported in a manner that will promote their objectives and not cause them trouble" while "the press wants news that will interest readers and viewers." Consequently, conflicting interests are present on both sides.

Today, community colleges face a crisis that is even more severe than dwindling enrollments and financial support: colleges lack the public's confidence in the quality of their product — education. In light of this situation (and in light of the public's right to remain informed about the institutions they support), it is extremely important for trustees to work effectively with the news media. Trustees must take the lead by understanding how the news media functions in a democratic society.

G. F. Petty (Ed.). *Active Trusteeship for a Changing Era.* New Directions for
Community Colleges, no. 51. San Francisco: Jossey-Bass, September 1985.

It is essential that the media and the trustees make up a team to satisfy the public's right to know as well as report on the many services and programs that community colleges have to offer. According to Movshovitz (1975), trustees should keep in mind the three "Cs" of media communication — continuity, candor, and consideration for mutually rewarding relationships. Controversy is indeed news and news reporters are more willing to help the colleges interpret crucial issues if college administrators or trustees initiate information.

Bagin, Grazian, and Harrison (1972) suggest that trustees: "Treat newsmen as you would like them to treat you. Respect the fact that they are trained professionals in their field just as you are in yours. Accept their right to probe into a college's budget to keep the public informed." Reporters who are on friendly terms with college sources generally will make every effort to be fair when controversy does develop. Helping them to meet their deadlines is also appreciated in times of controversy.

Protecting Your Institution's Image

The image of a community college is dependent on how the public perceives the college's progress and programs as well as how it handles problems. That image can be affected positively by many factors:

- Solid relationships with community and local press
- Open flow of information to and from the college
- The president acting as spokesperson for the college
- The trustee acting as goodwill ambassador to leadership and service organizations in the community.

Attitudes toward institutions are formed over time. The best defense against unfortunate publicity surrounding a crisis is a sustained program of media coverage. In addition to the media, newsletters, advisory committees, community services, open houses, and many other activities shape public opinion about your institution. The absence of a well coordinated program of public information invites a variety of impressions, many of which may be negative and may make the vital difference between success and failure in maintaining the mission of the institution.

For example, Oakton Community College, Illinois, has had successful relations with its fourteen surrounding communities by distributing weekly press releases. While there are pros and cons to this approach, Oakton has maintained an ongoing, consistent public information program by using nine suburban weekly and daily newspapers in their district of 100 square miles.

How does this program work? The community relations office writes ten to fifteen press releases per week conforming to Associated Press style and format. The releases are well written, cover a variety of topics, including specific features about students and faculty, and offer newspaper editors, who are short on help and working against deadlines, a consistent flow of information that needs no editing or rewriting. The releases can then be inserted as is into the paper. The press releases and photos are bundled up into fifteen different packets weekly and sent out by courier to each newspaper office. This ensures prompt delivery, and the results are worthwhile: a press release analysis shows 75 percent usage of releases in ten out of fifteen newspapers.

Packets of newsclips are collected weekly and sent to trustees, administrators, other newspapers, and selected community leaders. The clips show the wide variety of programs and services that Oakton has to offer and promotes the image of an active college responding to the needs of its community. The college and suburban newspapers have an ongoing cooperative partnership: the newspapers have a solution for personnel shortage and lack of educated reporters, and Oakton College receives high visibility and recognition.

Variables Affecting Image

Trustees and administrators should be concerned about their institution's image for three reasons (Kotler, 1982): (1) They need to know how their institution is perceived in relation to competing institutions; (2) they need to know how they are perceived by students, parents, and community leaders to maintain their continued support and enrollment; (3) they need to monitor any negative changes in image over time. Trustees should note Kotler's definition of image as "a set of beliefs that a person or group holds of an object or service."

How image is maintained or changed is dependent on many factors: good public relations programs, visible presidential leadership, and support of the trustees as goodwill ambassadors for the college's mission, policies, and programs. This is no easy task, but it certainly brings long term benefits to the college and to the community. The variables that affect a college's image are public opinion, the communicators of public opinion (the media), and the quality of the service provided by the college.

The news media is most influential in shaping the public image of the college. It affects the community's attitude toward the institution as well as the institution's sense of self worth. Reporters should be encouraged to attend all public board meetings. If nonpublic meetings of the board are allowed, these should be kept to a minimum and the presence of media representatives should be considered. If an understanding can be reached that reporters will only gather background information at nonpublic meetings, it is possible that confidentiality can be maintained.

Public information personnel on the college staff are a necessity. The news media should be well supplied with releases about college activities. So doing saves reporters time in obtaining the information and researching the facts and fills space or time for the media.

How much coverage any institution receives depends on numerous factors including size, quality of programs, cooperation among administrators and faculty, and the variety of newsmaking people and projects. Most important are the services of a competent public relations officer who is supported by an adequate staff, and trustees should heed the advice of this person. Many administrators and trustees who accept advice from their lawyers and physicians think nothing of ignoring advice about press relations when it comes from a public relations person.

It is also important to establish a policy of openness and candor in dealing with the press. One of the most valuable assets is having the confidence of members of the press. Nothing is more disconcerting than someone who tries to mislead a reporter by misstating facts, omitting pertinent information, or providing misleading information. A good reporter will check other sources and other trustees. It is the reporter's job to get the story that he feels the public has the right to know. It is usually more accurate if it comes from official sources rather than secondary sources. According to Ivey (1979), seven examples of communication barriers are: (1) secretiveness, (2) the "no comment" syndrome, (3) modesty, (4) fear of colleagues, (5) semantics (translating technical jargon into popular terms), (6) withholding information, and (7) intertia, fear of report selectivity.

Public Relations Policies

It is also important for trustees to approve a policy on communications that defines and guides actual practices. Conceiving and writing the policy can help educate trustees and other school officials. Both trustees and individual trustees have important roles to play in the implementation of the communication policy.

The board's duties and responsibilities are: (1) to see that the communications policy is implemented, (2) to communicate directly with the public through the board's open meeting, (3) to communicate directly with the public through appearances before school and civic organizations, and (4) to communicate directly with other governmental bodies and their members (for instance, state and national legislators). A note of caution: Board members must be careful to avoid usurping public relations duties of the president.

Role of the Chairman

Trustees who are not chairmen should realize that the relation between the college president and chairman is unique. There will be closer contact and understanding between the two than with the rest of the trustees. In cases of media intervention, the president must have direct access to the chairman for counsel and support when administrative decisions or interpretations of policy must be made. Some board members may feel left out if they are not sufficiently informed of significant decisions made or actions taken under such conditions. Board chairmen should communicate tactfully with the entire board to resolve such problems.

Communication is the key to good working relationships. All necessary information should be provided for review by the chair, who should share this information with the board as soon as possible. In some cases, a telephone pool of available board members is necessary. Like the chair, the other trustees should support their president publicly. By strengthening the president's image in the community, faculty, staff, and trustees will be justifying their good judgment in selecting him. A president's weaknesses should be compensated for by board strengths.

Trustees should also guard against dabbling in administration. The board sets policy but must allow the president to administer the policy. The board should also provide opportunities for the community to become acquainted with the president by organizing meetings.

Who Speaks for the College — Chairman or President?

Does the board chairman or college president speak for the college? This is a troublesome question. Some board members feel it is their right to speak for the college with the president acting as their administrative assistant. It is their view that they operate under a mandate from the voters and that they are thus legitimate institutional spokespersons. At other colleges, however, the president is looked upon as institutional leader and spokesperson. In any case, the question that all trustees must carefully consider before sharing information with the press is the question of institutional image. Anything that trustees say or hint at will affect public opinion about the college. In-service workshops should thus be a prerequisite for all trustees; such workshops should focus on the many facets of public opinion, community power structure, college marketing, and public perceptions of the college's program and administration.

Marketing the Message

Education is the biggest untold story in American journalism. Stories on education must compete with stories on rapes, fires, plane crashes, and political corruption. Editors do not want to hear what educators say unless it involves school closings, activist groups, strikes, or collective bargaining, and few reporters want to report on education.

The American media does an inadequate job of covering higher education, but educators must share at least part of the blame. It is important that trustees understand readers' perceptions before information is shared with news reporters. The first principle is that communication is a mutual act. In his speech to the Illinois chapter of the National School Public Relations Association in November, 1983, Patrick Jackson, former president of the Public Relations Society of America, suggests that only 20 percent of the people will remember your message if they only hear it; 30 percent if they hear and see it; 50 percent if they hear, see, and say it; and 90 percent if they hear, see, say, and do it. This is why it is important to get community constituents into the community college.

How does information travel? Diffusion theory explains the five steps a person goes through in the process of becoming convinced: (1) awareness, (2) interest or information seeking, (3) evaluation, (4) trial, and (5) decision. Communication is part of all five steps. However, in moving from step one to step five, the emphasis shifts from media communication to personal communication — from reading about it in the newspaper to talking to one's neighbor. This is why trustees cannot rely solely on media communication. There must be individuals who can personally tell the community college story.

How do community residents respond to this diffusion theory? According to Jackson, the following is true: 5 percent of the people will be zealously for your cause, 40 percent will be on your side, 10 percent will be undecided, 40 percent will be opposed, and 5 percent will be zealously against your cause. In order to have the majority favor your position, do not try to convince the opposition. Shape your messages for the 10 percent who are undecided. To share messages, do not stiffen resistance by asking for a willing suspension of disbelief. Emphasize the benefits and view the issue through the public's point of view, not the college's.

According to Kindred, Bagin, and Gallagher (1984), presenting only one side of an argument often causes readers to feel that they are being talked down to. Intellectual people with good educational backgrounds tend to be more influenced by two-sided messages, while persons of lesser intellectual ability tend to be influenced by one-sided messages. Further research has yielded conclusive findings about whether the opening or closing of a message should contain the more important content. By starting with a weaker point, an interested audience is more likely to be aroused when the important points are presented at the beginning (Kindred, Bagin, and Gallagher, 1984).

Trustees fail to realize that people tend to read, watch, and listen to communications that are in agreement with their beliefs and interests. They only hear or read what they expect to hear or read, rarely what the message says. People also remember the content of a message that supports what they believe more than they remember something antagonistic to their convictions. When few opinions have been formed, people will be more receptive to a well devised communication. When opinions are fixed and strongly defined, however, the chances of achieving attitude change are slight. Thus, it is better to work with existing attitudes by trying to slightly redirect them.

Trustee Actions and Strained Media Relations

It is not unusual that bad press can result from individual actions of board members. Some bad press may be the result of decisions made at regular board meetings. For example, if a bid procedure is violated and a distant vendor is approved over community vendors, public complaints will eventually come to the attention of the press. While controversial decisons may be inevitable in some cases, the board should plan strategies, do research, and provide statements for the press well in advance so that issues are met head on and the public is kept informed.

There are also individual trustees who play to the press for political or personal reasons. Instances of these types of trustees are identified below:

1. Trustees who invite reporters to a board meeting for a special self-interest agenda item.

2. Trustees who spring unexpected motions or statements on the floor that have little bearing on the business at hand.

3. Trustees who excuse themselves from the board table to speak to the press as a private citizen on a specific issue.

4. Trustees who leak an item to the press from executive sessions on personnel, real estate, or other sensitive matters.

5. Trustees who use the "Letters to the Editor" column in local papers to disclaim or rebut editorials and stories. (This can work both ways depending on the circumstances.)

6. Trustees who strive to get their names in the news, speak for a special interest group, or try to build up their egos.

7. Trustees who innocently make off the cuff comments on controversial matters over luncheons or cocktail parties; these comments can lead to distortions or misunderstandings.

From the above, one might get the impression that all actions of the board contribute to the negative side of media relations; this is not the case. Many boards engage in positive approaches to foster solid working relationships between the media and the college. These approaches include trustees initiating legislative breakfast or dinner meetings, being available for talk shows or to talk about school matters to service organizations, supporting college functions by being present, being knowledgeable about all school matters and progress, and aiding in organizing college/community support groups to visit the college.

Media representatives are also prone to call trustees at all hours to get their story. It is the job of a reporter to get the trustees to talk. It is not always the trustee's job to respond. Investigative reporters, part-time reporters, and reporters in transition are not eager to cover education unless some controversy surrounds it. Building rapport with a new reporter every three months is a difficult task for the public relations director, president, and trustees. Trustees should be prepared to support their position if they are in a minority voting on a major issue.

Guidelines for Dealing with the Media

Hartstein (1984) presents the following guidelines for solid, effective trustee-reporter relationships:

1. Attempt to influence the organizational structure at your colleges so that a high-level, competent public relations professional who understands the courting of public opinion is available to the president and others.

2. Be sure that the college has goals to be met in media relations and that the goals are regularly evaluated.

3. Make a communication audit of your own news clippings and other communications efforts to see what types of stories were generated from your releases and other efforts. This could involve a press release analysis on a monthly basis.

4. Identify all newspapers, radio, and public affairs programs that reach your intended audience.

5. Know what papers your reporters are affiliated with and the types of stories they have written. Update the list of reporters monthly. (The education beat is not the most popular one and loses reporters regularly.)

6. Do your utmost to understand the workings of media, its deadlines, and special requirements.

7. Become familiar with the freedom of information act and the open meetings law and realize that both foster a new openness in communications.

8. Try to inform the college of items that affect them before going to the press. If you are going to reduce staff, do not have the faculty learn of it from their neighbors or read about it in the local paper.

9. Release both good and bad news. Sometimes trustees will have to make unpopular decisions—closing down a worthwhile course due to small enrollments, limiting number of faculty because of the economic situation, and so on. This could result in negative press in either student or local newspapers. However, if trustees are open and honest in the way decisions are made, and have a reputation for dealing fairly with the media, an occasional negative story will not prove harmful.

10. Try not to be evasive or secretive. Evasiveness is a signal to the interviewer that you have something to hide. If trustees try to keep something a secret, one can be sure that it will be printed. For example, if you as trustees are going to release your president and either refuse to give the press any reasons why the action was taken or how it came about, you can be sure the press will play it for all it is worth, and the board and school will lose credibility.

11. Make no attempt to suppress news. If trustees do not cooperate with the press, rumors will gain prominence over fact. Then, too, suppressed news has a tendency to have more of a lasting effect and a more prominent play in the press.

12. Do your homework. Do it when you are not under pressure or in a stressful situation. Take time to brush up on current items on campus and recent news stories about the college.

64

13. Anticipate key questions, points of potential interest, hot spots or controversies well in advance.

14. Prepare answers to key questions you anticipate, including quotable quotes or phrases that present your answers in a catchy way. In addition to quotes, provide a reporter with some news if you can.

15. Tell the truth.

16. Avoid an argument with the reporter.

17. Resist any temptation to get you to attack others.

18. Challenge any effort to put words in your mouth, otherwise you may end up appearing to agree to the points you disagree with or admitting something you do not agree with.

19. Be sure the reporter knows when you are speaking off the record and advise him or her in advance.

20. If you cannot divulge information, state why in a matter-of-fact way.

21. If you don't know the answer to a question, say so and offer to find out the answer as soon as possible. Then provide the information to the interviewer. Always get back to a reporter if you committed yourself to do so.

Conclusion

In conclusion, one of the most important things a trustee can do to improve media relations is to do his or her job in the most rational, conscientious way possible and remember always to subordinate personal ego needs. If all the above is heeded, your trustees and your college should be a reliable, sought-after source of institutional information.

References

Bagin, D., Grazian, F., and Harrison, C. H. *School Communications: Ideas That Work. A Public Relations Handbook for School Officials.* Chicago: Nation's Schools Press, 1972.
Cutlip, S. M., and Center, A. H. *Effective Public Relations.* Englewood Cliffs, N.J.: Prentice-Hall, 1982.
Hartstein, R. "The Trustee and Media Relations." Des Plaines, Ill.: Oakton Community College, 1984.
Ivey, A. G. "Information Office Revisited." *College and University,* 1979, *12* (Fall), 27.
Jackson, P. Speech before the Illinois Chapter of the National School Public Relations Association, November, 1983.
Kindred, L., Bagin, D., and Gallagher, D. R. *School and Community Relations,* Englewood Cliffs, N.J.: Prentice-Hall, 1984.
Kotler, P. *Marketing for Nonprofit Organizations.* Englewood Cliffs, N.J.: Prentice-Hall 1982.

Movshovitz, H. *What Every School Board Member Should Know About Press and Community Relations*. Trenton, N.J.: New Jersey School Boards Association, 1975.

Jan Hamilton is former director of public relations, Oakton Community College, Des Plaines, Illinois.

Raymond Hartstein is a trustee at Oakton Community College in Des Plaines, Illinois.

*This chapter defines the proper role of trustees in the
accreditation process, suggests concrete and positive
approaches to trustee involvement, discusses factors that
negatively affect trustee participation, and recommends
future possibilities.*

The Trustee Role in Accreditation

Howard L. Simmons

Philosophically, at least, most agree that trustees are an important
constituent group in the community college and should therefore play an
active role in self-study, evaluation, and planning processes. More often
than not, the participation of trustees, except on a perfunctory basis, has
not been sought by the institutions themselves or by accrediting agencies. Even though we may agree that there are numerous ways to
actively involve trustees in these important aspects of higher education,
there are several reasons why community college trustees may not have
been actively involved including their own reluctance and the belief of
faculty, administrators, and accrediting officials that trustee involvement could lead to interference and overextension of trustee power. This
chapter defines the proper role of community college trustees in the
accreditation process, suggests concrete and positive ways for trustee
involvement, discusses factors that may negatively impact trustee participation, and recommends future possibilities.

For background, I have relied heavily on my own experiences as
a community college faculty member and administrator and as an
accrediting official. (This latter role has provided insights about two-
year college governance unobtainable in any other way. This is particularly important since research on this aspect of community college
governing boards is almost nonexistent.) Thus, many of the conclusions
reached are experientially based. Other useful resources on this topic are

G. F. Petty (Ed.). *Active Trusteeship for a Changing Era.* New Directions for
Community Colleges, no. 51. San Francisco: Jossey-Bass, September 1985.

The Board's Role in Accreditation (Association . . . ,1982) and *Functions of Boards and Trustees in Higher Education* (Commision . . . ,1984). In addition to having read numerous self-study and evaluation reports emphasizing trustee and college relationships, I have been fortunate in the middle states region to have interacted with trustees on almost every visit to community college campuses. It is important to add that representation of trustees at self-study/evaluation orientation sessions has been consistently high.

Rationale for Trustee Involvement

That an accreditation agency will take action on an institution's status following the self-study and evaluation processes becomes of less importance when one considers that the primary purpose for undertaking self-assessment should be institutional improvement. More important, the self-study is, or should be, only a part of the planning process — or the initial assessment phase — and should form the basis for further mission review, program planning, resource allocation, and the like. This is precisely the point at which community college trustees should exercise their greatest prerogative in the accreditation process, for it is in the planning process that basic decisions for the college are formulated, broad parameters are outlined, and overall priorities are established. Zwingle (1975) concludes: "Disengaged from the daily demands of operations and the daily pressures of individuals and groups, the board is in a position to press for priorities, both short-term and long-term" (p. 31).

It is unlikely that the self-study process on campus can be considered really successful should there not be some assurance on the part of those involved that resulting recommendations will be carefully considered or at least have some basis in reality. It does no good to complete a self-study report that is at variance with the priorities established by the board of trustees. Since these priorities are usually found in strategic and long-range planning documents, it is logical that trustees be significantly and actively involved on institutional planning committees or task forces. Further, there should be some formal relationship between the institutional planning group and the self-study steering committee, thereby providing additional opportunity for trustees to participate actively in the accreditation process.

The Trustees' Role

What is the proper role of community college trustees in the institutional self-study process? Clearly, most trustees do not feel compelled or consider it appropriate to serve personally on institutional self-study steering committees and work groups. Moreover, some trustees and other college constituent groups (faculty and administrators) are concerned that such involvement might result in a less candid self-study report, or at least cause other participants to feel intimidated, particularly at those institutions where some trustees are already perceived to be overly involved in the day-to-day administration of the college. Potter (1976), who assesses the proper role of the board, argues that "the effective board insists on being the policymaker for all aspects of institutional life but refuses to meddle in the administration of the college" (p. 2). However, some campuses have welcomed active trustee participation in these groups and have been aware of the useful perspectives provided by trustees, particularly with respect to community needs, public relations and image, placement opportunities for students, availability of resources, and so on. Obviously, the degree and level of trustee participation involves a number of factors, depending on the institution: (1) the degree of trustee knowledge of and interest in the self-study activity, (2) the form of college governance, (3) the quality of relations between trustees and faculty/staff, and (4) the form of self-study. Experience in the middle states region suggests that real involvement of community college trustees is inherent in self-study processes; trustees are regularly informed of the study's progress and have an opportunity to review the final report before it is submitted to accrediting bodies, evaluation teams, and other appropriate bodies.

Even though not all community college trustees will have the opportunity to participate fully in general institutional self-study processes, there is absolutely no reason why trustees should not carry out an appraisal of their own effectiveness, or of the college itself. The former president of the Association of Governing Boards (Zwingle, 1975) agrees: "Whereas the accrediting bodies give a periodic audit of the academic quality of an institution, only the governing board can invite an audit of itself and the total health of the institution" (p. 14).

Indeed, effective community college trustees are recognizing the value of appraising their own performance and accountability in a more systematic way by use of an evaluation instrument. Obviously, such self-assessments can be carried out by utilizing both commercially prepared and inhouse instruments. Even though the interested community college boards wants the most reliable data for its analysis, the form of the instrument should be less important than the rationale for carrying out the self-evaluation procedures. Polk and Coleman (1976) emphasize that the instrument need not be complex and should be "designed primarily to stimulate thought among the board members . . . ." Those trustee boards seeking to implement such a program of self-evaluation should get assistance from groups such as the Association of Community College Trustees (ACCT), the Association of Governing Boards (AGB), state or regional community college trustee groups, or regional accrediting bodies.

One widely used instrument is the AGB *Self-Study Guidelines and Criteria for Governing Boards of Community Colleges*, whose administration and analysis are usually followed by a workshop or retreat so that a full discussion of the findings and implications can be realized by all trustees. Since this instrument also assesses the board members' relationships with other college constituent groups and their perceptions of the college's interaction with the community, it nicely complements the college's self-study process. A careful analysis of the results usually indicates whether board adopted policies are being implemented and whether the board is fully aware of the college's administrative and academic functions. Further, the results of the self-assessment can be used by the board in institutional planning and in formulating future policy.

Now that the internal evaluations and assessments have been completed prior to an evaluation visit, the board of trustees should become actively involved in reviewing the self-study report before it is submitted to external groups. It should be emphasized that the review does not give the board license to unilaterally tamper with or make alterations in a document that has been prepared previously by faculty, administrators, and students. Rather, it suggests an opportunity for the board to examine the document in light of the college's mission, resources, outcomes, and board policies. Such a review — to be followed by suggestions, if any, to the campus steering committee — should be conducted through the office of the president and should at no time give the appearance that the board wishes to substitute its judgment for that of the college's steering group on which trustees may have had representation.

That the self-study process and its results are usually viewed as an important phase of the institution's continuous planning process is even more reason why the board should make every effort to utilize the results of the self-assessment to expand, contract, or reorder its priorities, or to revise old policies and formulate new policy. As long as follow-up of self-study recommendations also involves other constituent groups via the college's governance structure, the trustees should be well able to provide significant input at this stage of the accreditation process. While actual reviews of planning processes will depend on individual institutional circumstances, the reviews should involve, at minimum, the board's committee on academic affairs or a standing committee on planning. What has been described or suggested to this point assumes that the full board has been periodically informed of the progress of the self-study by the chief executive officer (CEO) or the CEO's designee. The final report should be discussed fully at a regular or plenary session of the board so that every trustee will not only be aware of its contents but will understand the rationale for recommendations, especially in areas where the college may not have met its goals and objectives or may be in serious noncompliance with the standards or policies of the accrediting body.

Having readied itself for the evaluation team visit, the college must ensure that the trustees continue to be active participants in the process. Aside from formal orientation activities that occur at the outset of the visit, there is an absolute need for the trustees — especially in the community college — to meet with the team or its chair during the visit so that the trustees' perceptions of the college and their visions of the college's future growth and development can be captured. As for the team, this meeting provides an opportunity to determine whether the board fully understands its role, is supportive of the college's mission, and is adequately informed of the college's strengths, concerns, and prospects. Provided the meeting is conducted properly and the right inquiries are made by the trustees and the team, the experience can be quite valuable to both groups. For example, the trustees may learn more about the value of self-study and the accreditation process and the team members may become better acquainted with the college's governance system and the quality of institutional decision making. Finally, the board should be represented at the exit conference, even if all members cannot be present to hear the team's findings. Aside from being able to get the results directly, the board may be appraised of deficiencies that are in its domain to correct even before the final report of the team is received by the college or before action is taken on the college's accreditation status. Once the final team's report is received, however, it is the board's responsibility to review the report and to make suggestions to the present for possible inclusion in the institution's response, particularly where the report speaks directly to the board and its role and functions.

Even after the college has received the accrediting body's notification of status, the board's involvement is not over. The board must work with the president in responding to major recommendations and in determining how the evaluation results will affect current and future priorities.

Other Areas of Board Involvement

How else might community college trustees be actively involved in the accreditation process? First, they may be requested by accrediting bodies to serve on visiting teams, on special committees or commissions, or as consultants. Community college trustees who have had significant experience in self-study and assessment can serve as consultants to other boards and either assist in the resolution of specific problems or provide general orientation to new board members. Since most of the new trustees will not have had any previous experience with the accreditation process, this service will be invaluable to their more complete understanding of the college's mission, goals, and objectives and to how these relate to outcomes and the accrediting agency standards. Moreover, trustees can be given realistic and concrete examples about expected behavior of trustees and how effective stewardship can be maintained at the highest professional level.

Second, community college trustees can attend regular and special meetings of accrediting bodies in order to become better informed about the conduct and rules of the agency. Besides becoming more knowledgeable about the policies and standards of the accrediting bodies, the trustees become aware of the difference between the need for quality and accountability and the need to protect the institution's autonomy, especially when the agency becomes overly prescriptive. This is not to imply that this is a problem but rather to suggest that trustees should be aware of the institution's rights and responsibilities in the accreditation process.

Third, community college boards must be cognizant of college involvement in programmatic reviews other than the regional or institutional self-studies. While it is the president's responsibility to keep trustees informed of the review schedule and rationale for it, trustees should be proactive in getting this type of information. Naturally, accreditation reviews are not conducted without cost to the college; thus, the trustees should understand what impact the reviews will have on the budget. The key question to be considered by the trustees will be whether this particular evaluation and the accreditation process results in improvements in the institution's quality and outcomes. In most cases, the answer will be in the affirmative and the funds for self-study and evaluation will have been well spent, especially when benefits accrue to both the institution and its students. Thus, financial considerations should not be the deciding factor as to whether or not a particular form of accreditation is sought.

Finally, trustees in the community college can become goodwill ambassadors helping community groups and the public at large understand the college's mission and outcomes and ultimately how the accreditation process serves as a factor in the improvement of the college.

To summarize, community college trustees can be actively involved in the accreditation process in numerous ways, including:

1. Being active participants in reviewing the college's mission, goals and objectives;
2. Making a strong commitment to continuous institutional planning, strategic and long range;
3. Participating, where appropriate, on self-study steering committees and special work groups related to trustee concerns (governance);
4. Conducting their own self-evaluation and internal institutional assessments;
5. Meeting with evaluation and review teams to provide the board's perspective;
6. Attending the exit interview conducted by evaluation teams;
7. Participating on evaluation teams, as appropriate;
8. Attending workshops and conferences on accreditation sponsored by accrediting bodies and other groups, including ACCT and AGB;
9. Keeping abreast of the institution's involvement with the total range of accrediting activities, including both institutional and specialized reviews; and
10. Promoting the value and meaning of accreditation to the community and the public at large.

At any point in the accreditation process, the board member's involvement should be related to her or his right and need to be informed about important issues facing voluntary accreditation itself, community colleges in particular, and higher education in general. As a major constituent group of the college, trustees must be active participants in keeping with their role.

References

Association of Government Boards. *The Board's Role in Accreditation*. Washington, D.C.: Association of Governing Boards, 1982.

Commission on Higher Education, Middle States Association. *Functions of Boards of Trustees in Higher Education*. Commission on Higher Education, Philadelphia: 1984.

Polk, C. H., and Coleman, H. C., Jr. "Self-Evaluation, Key to Accountability." In V. Dziuba and W. Meardy (Eds.), *Enhancing Trustee Effectiveness*, New Directions for Community Colleges, no. 15. San Francisco: Jossey-Bass, 1976. 109 pp. (ED 130 693)

Potter, G. E. "Responsibilities." In V. Dziuba and W. Meardy (Eds.), *Enhancing Trustee Effectiveness*, New Directions for Community Colleges, no. 15. San Francisco: Jossey-Bass, 1976. 109 pp. (ED 130 693)

Zwingle, J. L. *Effective Trusteeship*, Washington, D.C.: Association of Governing Boards, 1975.

Howard L. Simmons is associate director of the Commission of Higher Education, Middle State Association of Schools and Colleges, Philadelphia, Pennsylvania.

Trustees play an important role in leading the institution to
positive, productive collective bargaining procedures.

Trustees and Collective Bargaining

Robert V. Moriarty

For more than a century, public education in America has witnessed the
rise of teachers' organizations and their evolution into unions. By 1972,
the total number of teachers in the elementary and secondary schools
had increased over 265 percent since 1944, and nearly two-thirds of these
teachers belonged to the American Federation of Teachers (AFT) or the
National Education Association (NEA) (Moore and Marshall, 1973).

Similarly, the public community colleges and technical institutes
experienced a dramatic increase in the number of teachers employed as
well as in their affiliation with teachers' unions. In New York in 1972, for
example, 119 of the 158 separate bargaining units in higher education
were involved in community colleges (Duryea and others, 1973). By
1982, over one-half of the community college districts in Illinois were
engaged in collective bargaining. More than 90 percent of the faculty
teaching in these districts were recognized by either the AFT, the NEA,
or affiliates (Marzano, 1984).

However dramatic the increase in teachers' unionization has
appeared since World War II, it pales in comparison to the expansion of
bargaining units in response to state statutes over the last ten years that
mandate collective bargaining for the employees of public community
colleges. For example, in New York, 90 percent of all community colleges
were organized within five years of the passage of such laws (Duryea and
others, 1973). Further, with the passage of such laws effective in Illinois

G. F. Petty (Ed.). *Active Trusteeship for a Changing Era*. New Directions for
Community Colleges, no. 51. San Francisco: Jossey-Bass, September 1985.

in 1984, almost all districts are attempting to negotiate with a collective bargaining unit.

In many cases, such negotiating rights have been extended to, and claimed by, nonfaculty, including technical, clerical, and other support employees.

On a national scale never before experienced, trustees have had, at this time in public community college history, to deal with the technically demanding, time consuming, unpredictable, and emotionally draining process of collective bargaining with faculty and other groups of employees.

Activist Trustees

The negotiations process has all the allure and potential consequences of a flame for a moth for those activist trustees who fail to acquire an appropriate perspective on this process, who are unclear or unsure as to the trustee role, and who are unwilling to become involved in the essential planning for the process. Trustees must understand how collective bargaining at community colleges differs from collective bargaining at other institutions in the public and private sectors. Further, trustees must understand the enormous impact collective bargaining can have on the dynamic relationship among trustees, faculty, administration, students, and community. The quality of that relationship can be either enhanced or vitiated by the collective bargaining process, and the behaviors and attitudes of trustees — as perceived by other parties in the negotiations — are the most critical elements in campus collective bargaining.

The bargaining process has significant potential for impact, both positive and negative, on the general psychological health, economic security, and instructional vitality of community colleges. This chapter presents a model of the way in which a community college, under the leadership of its board and with the cooperation of other players in the system, can effect a workable collective bargaining agreement without potentially disruptive behavior and can bring an increased sense of commitment and responsibility to the college.

Distributive Versus Integrative Approach

It is likely that, before the end of this decade, the overwhelming majority of public community colleges will be involved in collective bargaining. Districts will either employ under-prepared administrators or outside negotiators; this has been described as the distributive approach to negotiations. This approach, the most traditional and pervasive in the private sector, assumes that the parties involved in negotiations are adversarial, that their goals are in conflict with each other, and that one party's gain is the other party's loss (Millerick, 1983).

While the negotiations process is potentially a way of problem solving or conflict resolution, the assumptions of the distributive approach all too often make collective bargaining part of the problem rather than the solution. Communications become more limited and are more manipulative rather than informative. Real interests are hidden, while attempts are made to mislead. Information becomes more and more distorted as attempts at manipulation increase and positions rigidify. Constructive dispute becomes disruptive, cooperation is inhibited, and aggressive, confrontive behavior increases. As one researcher noted, the traditional approach to bargaining in an era of dwindling resources suggests that campuses "shall be fighting more and more over less and less" (Birnbaum, 1983).

The picture painted is admittedly grim but not exaggerated. In one respect it is incomplete, for it does not include the eventual outcome of organizational dysfunction—the strike. Those trustees who have experienced the agony of a college under strike have regretted the hostility, bitterness, disrespect, indignation, and confusion of the community.

The antithesis of the distributive approach to bargaining is integrative bargaining or principled negotiations. This approach is predicated on an assumption of genuine interest in the mutual exploration of problems, joint fact finding, and joint problem solving (Millerick, 1983). Several professional studies support the validity and effectiveness of this approach. Millerick describes the Harvard Negotiation Project report, *Getting to Yes*, that evaluates this approach as a workable, straightforward method for the negotiation of disputes "without getting taken — and without getting nasty" (Millerick, 1983, p. 38).

Integrative bargaining provides the philosophical assumptions as well as the general context in which negotiations can occur. It underscores the premise that the parties to a collective bargaining agreement—the board and its administrative agents and the union and its member faculty—have a common area of interest. This shared goal is the creation and maintenance of an environment wherein the highest quality of instructional service can be provided in an efficient and effective manner by professionals who are sufficiently supported and appropriately cooperative.

The Creative Use of Neutrals

Although the integrative approach provides a necessary foundation, it is not in itself a sufficient condition for productive negotiations. The other necessary element is the use of neutrals. Neutrals are professional facilitators who .are experienced with the issues and jargon of public community colleges. Traditionally, neutrals (or mediators) would not be involved in the negotiations process until an impasse had been reached between the parties. In this proposed model, neutrals would be involved from the beginning of the planning phase. These neutrals would be selected jointly by board and union and both their fees and expenses would be shared by both parties.

This approach to collective bargaining in a community college is not without precedent. The Institute of Higher Education at Teachers College, Columbia University, conducted an experimental test of this approach at Atlantic Community College in 1981 (Birnbaum, 1983). Despite (or perhaps because of) a long history of bitter and contentious contract bargaining using the traditional approach, both parties were willing to attempt a radically different approach to negotiations. Beginning with prenegotiations data gathering, the neutral surveyed numerous faculty, administrators, and board members in order to identify their perceptions of the organization's problems. The neutral then structured a workshop for all parties to receive feedback from the survey and to brainstorm possible solutions. The workshop was characterized by an evolving sense of understanding of the other side's position and was achieved in a nonadversarial environment.

With the commencement of formal negotiations, the neutral became a consultant on the bargaining process. For example, the neutral was able to identify potential areas of agreement and point these out to both sides. Having attended all formal sessions as well as having been present for all caucuses of both sides, the neutral was able to help the parties understand the proposals and counterproposals and their real implications.

After successful negotiations of nonmonetary matters, issues related to salaries and fringe benefits were discussed. At this point, the former disruptive, antagonistic behavior emerged and resulted in an impasse. Since the neutral had established a relationship with both parties, he was able to assume the role of formal mediator and successfully assist the parties in reaching an agreement. Followup evaluation of the project indicated that significant attitudinal changes as well as improvements in communications had occurred between the parties (Millerick, 1983).

The Atlantic Community College project is a study of the comprehensive utilization of a neutral in the negotiations process. There are other examples of the successful employment of a third party neutral in collective bargaining at other levels of education.

The Win-Win Approach

An illustration of a more stylized and structured approach to the third party neutral in collective bargaining of particular relevance to trustees is found in the model developed by Irving Goldaber, a noted sociologist specializing in conflict management (Moriarty, 1984). The Goldaber model, described as a win-win approach to collective bargaining, is based upon the concept of shared goals in contrast to the traditional, distributive model of opposing values. In this model, the survival and best interest of the district as a whole are the logical shared goal of both the union and the board.

This approach requires the formal adoption by both parties of various protocols or rules that govern the entire bargaining process. These protocols underscore the cooperative mode of this approach, focusing on the interaction between the actual parties to the agreement, that is, the entire board and the employee representatives. Administrators, as well as external union representatives and legal counsel for both parties, serve only as resource persons. The protocols typically prescribe an intensive, weekend-long discussion on all concerns expressed by the board and by the union. For the ensuing three weeks, joint board-union committees consider those concerns in depth, with the goal of reaching resolution within the committees. The process is completed at another intensive weekend session, at which time the agreements and any unresolved matters are reviewed. The parties have agreed to consider all issues until a contract is achieved. The probability of this outcome is increased, since joint-board-union committees have already reached implicit agreement.

This approach to negotiations rests on significantly nontraditional bargaining concepts: dramatically changed roles of board members, administrators, and board attorney; a prearranged time frame; mutual commitment to that time frame as well as to cooperation; and the involvement of a neutral facilitator.

Conclusion

Because collective bargaining has become a reality for trustees in the 1980s and because trustees want to effect negotiated contracts that enable the board to fulfill its fiduciary responsibilities while at the same time preserving the spirit, vitality, and commitment of college employees, the activitist trustee must carefully consider alternative approaches to negotiations. The potential advantages of the utilization of neutrals in the entire process of negotiations are indeed compelling, as the following demonstrates:

1. Trustees who are legally responsible for the outcome (the contract) are actively involved in the process in a functional manner.

2. Even in institutions that have a history of bitter, adversarial bargaining replete with work stoppages and other hostile, destructive behavior, skilled neutral facilitators can effect increased cooperation and mutual respect among the board and its employees. An improved climate for learning probably occurs as well.

3. In addition to a more mutually beneficial outcome, the parties involved in the process learn more effective ways of problem solving, a benefit that extends beyond the achievement of a contract.

4. There is every indication that when a board and an employee group share the cost of a neutral facilitator, the major expense of negotiations is significantly reduced as compared to the cost of hiring a professional negotiator for a traditional, adversarial process.

The decade of the 1980s has brought new challenges and problems to college trustees. The best interests of community colleges demand that trustees look beyond old approaches and traditional methods.

References

Birnbaum, R. "Making Faculty Bargaining Work." *Educational Record*, 1983, *64* (3), 37–39.

Duryea, E. D., Fisk, R., and associates. *Faculty, Unions, and Collective Bargaining*. San Francisco: Jossey-Bass, 1973.

Marzano, W. A. "Formalization of Faculty Working Conditions in Illinois Public Community Colleges." Unpublished doctoral dissertation, Illinois State University, 1984.

Millerick, M. "Negotiations and Fringe Benefits." *Thrust*, 1983, 13 (3), 37, 38.

Moore, W. J., and Marshall, R. "Growth of Teacher's Organizations: A Conceptual Framework." *Journal of Collective Negotiations in the Public Sector*, 1973, *2* (3), 272.

Moriarty, K. M. "Alternative Approach to Agreement: A Possibility When Trust Has Evaporated." *ANCA Reports*, 1984, *1* (November), 5.

Robert V. Moriarty is president of the Forest Institute of Professional Psychology in Des Plaines, Illinois.

The effective chairperson must always emphasize the best interests of the institution.

The Effective Chairperson

Peter Lardner

The chair of a board of trustees may be either help or hindrance in respect to college governance. At issue is the chairperson's leadership quality. This chapter presents some theories about effective leadership, examines efforts to classify leadership styles, and makes some pragmatic observations about the application of leadership theories and styles to the community college setting.

Differences in the Leadership Role of the Chairperson

The leadership role of the chair differs from other leadership situations. The board chair is typically elected by peers. In contrast, military commanders or business leaders reach their positions (for the most part) through a non-selective process. (An exception is the corporate chief executive officer or board chair who is elected by corporate board members.) This nondemocratic process is the norm for corporations or the military.

How authority is achieved is important, because the style and character of leadership is molded by the environment in which leadership is exercised. A naval captain in a combat situation or a corporate executive in a hostile business environment are both in different settings than the chair of a board of trustees of a community college. The latter

G. F. Petty (Ed.). *Active Trusteeship for a Changing Era*. New Directions for Community Colleges, no. 51. San Francisco: Jossey-Bass, September 1985.

owes authority to the decisions of a peer group whose members have equal voting rights with the chair and whose cooperation and consensus are needed for effective action. With that difference in mind, a consideration of leadership characteristics and styles can be helpful in analyzing leadership effectiveness of the board chair.

The Chairperson as an Interlocutor

Despite the enormous attention the topic of leadership has received in the literature, Luthans (1981) concludes that leadership is still an unexplainable concept or "black box." He acknowledges pioneer studies on the nature of leadership, but argues that these studies suggest that it is as important to understand the nature of the group being led as it is to understand the style of the leader. Reflecting upon theories of leadership, Luthans concludes that "leadership is an exchange process between the leaders and followers" and involves the expectations that both parties bring to the situation. He asserts that "leaders who take into account and support their followers have a positive impact upon attitudes, satisfaction, and performance" (pp. 413–419).

Thus, the chair of a community college board of trustees should be the go-between, the interlocutor. The chair must take into account the concerns of all affected by or involved with board actions; these parties include not only fellow board members but also students, staff, faculty, and administrators. This task requires mediation skills. The expectations of faculty may often conflict with the expectations of administration; demands for higher salaries, for example, may arise at the same time administrators are trying to cut or balance the budget. Another common conflict stems from student demands for increased course offerings in the face of faculty demands for reasonable teaching loads. The chairperson needs to contain this conflict and to steer opposing parties towards outcomes that are in the best interest of the institution.

This is not easily done. Consider, for example, the often volatile atmosphere of public meetings, during which the chair is most visible and most vulnerable. Public meetings tempt the chair to respond in the heat of the moment rather than for the good of the institution as a whole. People chairing trustee meetings have, at times, been interrupted by demonstrating faculty who, wielding placards, call out demands and draw attention to their cause by rude interruptions. Tempted as the chair may be to respond humanly and abruptly, the chair does well to subordinate this response to the best interest of the college. How does one support a seemingly hostile faculty? Without support, how can the faculty respond to the leadership of the chair?

Consider that a proposal is made to raise tuition, perhaps with the goal to provide fair salaries for faculty. Such a proposal is likely to draw a good turnout of students, probably of varied ages, who will consider the proposal unjust. They will plead that a tuition hike may well doom an entire generation of would-be students to a life of unemployed bleakness without the benefit of education. The chair may be tempted to counter with emotion and energy and disregard the best interests of the institution. How does a chair support students while at the same time supporting other constituencies in the college committee?

Even the administration, with whom the chair is usually closest, may on occasion test the vision and discipline of the chair. Occasionally, a clumsy administrator gives the board an inadequate presentation of an ill-thought-out proposal that is unjustified by any standard. While the chair may be tempted to ridicule or castigate, such action undermines support, and, at such a moment, support is what the administration needs.

Fellow board members are among those who are most cooperative when supported by the chair. What does the chair do when a fellow trustee becomes personally attacking, accusatory, and seems intent on destroying an orderly public meeting? At such times the chair does well to take a deep breath, count slowly to ten, and remember that what is at stake is the best interests of the institution. Despite the temptation to meet fire with fire, the chair must protect the institution and all of its constituents, even including those who may be part of the problem. To be constructive in a public meeting, the chair must recognize rhetoric for what it is: dry tinder that is easily ignitable and that has highly destructive consequences for the meeting and for the institution. The chair should buffer the institution from rhetoric and be an inexhaustible source of coolness, calmness, and firmness. At stake is nothing less than institutional progress that will be jeopardized if the participants satisfy selfish interests.

Approaches to Board Leadership

Good leadership may involve taking into account and supporting one's followers, as Luthans proposes. But what about specific approaches that might enhance the effectiveness of the board chair? Many theories and studies of leadership focus on production situations and contrast the leader's emphasis on persons involved with the emphasis on the product produced. Blake and Moulton (1981), for instance, have developed a managerial grid that evaluates leadership in terms of varying emphases on people and production. While such theories may be applicable to factories, they are hard to apply to the leadership role exercised by the community college board chairperson. Board productivity could be thought of as the ability to move through an agenda efficiently and quickly. However, analogy between board activities and factory production of measurable products is weak.

Group performance is determined by a combination of leadership style and the circumstances. Research suggests that a task-directed or hard nosed type of leader is the most effective in either favorable or unfavorable situations. However, for situations that are only moderately favorable or unfavorable, a lenient type of leader is most effective. Translating this to a community college board setting, one might conclude that, in a crisis (or in a meeting where the proper course of action is self-evident) a directive style of leadership may be most productive. But the issues addressed at most board meetings are not always clear cut. Studies support the argument that the chair's best approach to leadership is considerate behavior toward other board members, administrators, faculty, students, and all other college constituents.

One way a chair can be considerate or supportive is to let other people do their jobs. A supportive chair lets the president do the president's job. This includes letting the president represent and speak for the position of the president. Similarly, the chair should let other officers represent and speak for their positions. Other trustees also have roles and should have the opportunity to perform these roles. They should be heard and respected.

The public also should be given an opportunity to play a full role in the work of the board, and the chair is the best person to see that that happens. The chair should always see that the public's view is represented at the meeting. Even if the chair has to state a question for the public or challenge the board itself from the standpoint of the public, the public view should be represented.

Thus, the strategy for facilitating good outcomes for the institution is for the chair to represent every party and to guarantee all parties have a chance to be heard and to participate. Good processes often produce good outcomes, and the process of a meeting is the responsibility of the chair.

A particular responsibility of the chair is to work closely with the president, with the chair serving as coach, sounding board, ally, and associate. In this way, the chair contributes toward a supportive and productive environment. The chair should question the president before meetings about agenda topics. What will the president's position be? How will the president state and support that view? Will the subordinates of the president participate in the board presentation? How? Is there consistency between the president and the staff? If not, what is the problem? What is the stance at the meeting going to be? Who is going to make the presentation and provide the explanations? Will the explanations be adequate? In these preliminary discussions, the chair should anticipate what other board members will ask and what they will challenge or support. Unexpected opposition to the administration may be good copy for reporters but it is trouble for the institution. If the chair expects to differ in public with the president, the chair must inform the president ahead of time. The best prevention for troublesome surprises is preparation — full explanations, good homework, and sensitivity by the chair toward all trustees and other constituencies of the college.

How does a good chair handle the public meeting of the board? The effective chair seeks to control the meeting not to dominate it. No group can do business well with a passive chair. When chairing a meeting, as when chairing the board, the chair should not be a spectator but an active participant. A chair should not abrogate responsibility to the president or anyone else. Nor should a fellow board member become an ad hoc chair when the designated chair is present. The chair should work for balance in discussing the pros and cons of the issues. The chair has an obligation to cultivate an atmosphere that supports and encourages full and fair discussion. The chair should ask those questions that should be asked and should also restate questions that are unclear until the original questioner agrees the intent is being stated clearly. The chairperson also has a responsibility to stop filibusters by board members, president, faculty, or members of the public.

At the same time, the chair should be careful and judicious in making statements. The chair should never abuse the power to influence others by putting words in others' mouths or to force ideas upon fellow trustees. The power of the chair should be spent frugally and conserved thoughtfully.

Finally, every trustee and especially the chair, should work to retain and exercise a sense of humor. Humor and perspective can help smooth the most tangled meeting. One can always reflect that, in a hundred years of meetings, few historians will care much about what happened at any one session. That humbling thought helps retain perspective and can reduce many problems to a manageable size.

References

Blake, R. R. "Managerial Facades." *Advanced Management*, 4 (July), 31.
Luthans, F. *Organizational Behavior*. New York: McGraw-Hill, 1981.

Peter Lardner is a trustee at Black Hawk College in Illinois.

The board has an important role to play in determining personnel management policies.

The Trustee Role in College Personnel Management

Clem R. Jasiek
Alfred Wisgoski
Hans A. Andrews

The board's role in hiring and firing is an issue that is so sensitive and misunderstood that no one wants to mention it. There is no greater responsibility of a board of trustees than personnel management. Between 80 and 85 percent of many college budgets go to personnel salaries and fringe benefits.

It is in this area that board policies can make or break the effectiveness of any institution. Strong and clearly defined board policies, closely adhered to by the board and its administrative personnel, can provide the framework for producing a quality institution.

The essential ingredients for effective recruitment, retention, or dismissal of college personnel are: (1) a strong governing board, (2) a strong president and staff, (3) mutual support, and (4) clearly defined personnel policies and procedures. Any attempt to establish an effective personnel system, no matter how well conceived or well intentioned, is doomed to failure if any one of these essential ingredients is lacking. Given a strong board, president, and staff, a systematic plan for personnel recruitment, retention, and dismissal should be adopted as board

G. F. Petty (Ed.). *Active Trusteeship for a Changing Era.* New Directions for Community Colleges, no. 51. San Francisco: Jossey-Bass, September 1985.

policy. This plan can provide the basis for the president and his staff to continuously monitor both quality and need.

Guaranteeing Quality

There are actions a board of trustees can take that will help guarantee quality. Some of these are:

1. Provide the institution with a high quality president who is well educated, experienced, and committed to the objectives of the institution;

2. Have a policy of open job searches for all other administrators and faculty members;

3. Develop a policy on evaluation that guarantees close supervision and scrutiny of administration and faculty during initial and non-tenure years;

4. Reserve tenure appointments for only the very best;

5. Expect remediation for poor performances from tenured faculty; and

6. Be willing to fire incompetent staff (administrative or faculty).

Establishing Values

Underlying the above measures should be a commitment to the values that will guide the institution. These values may be long term historical values or they may be values that have evolved during a twenty to thirty year growth period.

Some of these values should include: (1) excellence in instruction; (2) a strong administrative/board team approach to problem solving; (3) a commitment to helping community organizations, agencies, businesses, and industries with their educational needs; (4) fiscal responsibility.

The values of the institution, as reflected by its board of trustees, should be the driving force behind board policies, program development, college budgets and audits, and personnel decisions on hiring, retention, and dismissal.

One of the strongest commitments that trustees in any institution can make is to clarify institutional values. What is important? What institutional characteristics can be used to evaluate trustee and staff effectiveness?

The major mission of community colleges is instruction. It is natural, therefore, that boards place a high value on quality instruction.

The success of transfer students to four-year colleges, the successful placement in jobs of technical students, and the meaningful interaction of the community college with business, industry, and community agencies are goals that can give a board a sense of meaning and direction. Clarification of values also helps to set a framework for all other requirements, tasks, and actions the board will be called on to perform.

Quality instruction necessitates hiring qualified and competent faculty members, maintaining reasonable class sizes, and providing adequate class supplies and reasonably modern instructional equipment. It also means maintaining competitive salaries for faculty, support staff, and administrators. The budget for the college should be passed after the matters of maintaining quality instruction (and other areas the board considers as values) have been addressed.

Values can give meaningful direction to the board, they can reinforce decisions made by the board to agenda items recommended by the president and staff, and they can help keep a board and a college on course.

A well maintained campus and facilities, a balanced budget and high community and state visibility are other areas likely to be designated valuable.

Hiring Personnel: The President's Role

Community college trusteeship can and should have a reasonable degree of prestige. Trustees in most states are elected by the district constituency or appointed by the governor of the state. How much and how far ranging the prestige will be is very definitely related to the quality of personnel the board hires.

The selection of personnel is and should be a competitive process. In selecting the college president, there will be competition between candidates. There may also be competition between two or more colleges that are interested in the same candidate. A board can take pride and satisfaction when it hires a president who will adequately carry out the missions of the college within the policy framework established by the local board and the state.

It is important that there be agreement on the meaning of excellence among the board members. Lacking this, it will be difficult for the chief executive officer to pursue the goals of the board. The president should be accountable to the board but should understand the goals to be met. The board should know what excellence in education means and be willing to pursue that goal.

McGrath (1977) views the main function of a board of trustees as helping set the basic policies of the college, monitoring how those policies are carried out, remaining informed on all significant aspects of the institution's operation, and assuring that the chief executive has integrity and enjoys their confidence.

Kauffman (1983) states that ". . . there are many universal things that can be said about governing boards and presidents. Foremost would be that neither can be effective without the other. Certainly the president must be successful in his/her relationship with the governing board in order to function" (p. 18).

The president's relationship to the board and the chairperson is vital in a functional and organizational sense as well as a personal and career sense. The authority of a president is enhanced by a board that insists on approving major policy and fiscal matters, including tenure.

When important decisions are subject to review, the president can utilize the board's involvement as a reason to resist pressures for a questionable action. As Kauffman comments, "if it is known that the board will have to be provided with evidence and the rationale for any recommendation, that a specific recommendation from the chief executive officer will have to be made, it becomes difficult for special interests to precipitate unwise actions" (p. 19).

Trustees should understand that a president must also consider the expectations and traditions of faculty, staff, and students and cannot merely carry out the board's orders. It should be seen as a sign of strength when a president is concerned with the interests of all constituent groups as well as the governing board.

The Board's Powers in Personnel Management

The powers and duties of a board are often better known in law and in courts than by individual board members. Piele (1980) states that "It is a well settled rule of law that boards of education have only those powers that are expressly granted or reasonably inferred to them by the legislature of the state or that have been granted to the board of education through the state board of education by rule or regulation" (p. 8). Such power or authority cannot and should not be delegated.

The courts find that board of education policies will carry "the same weight of authority as state law within the confines of the school district. Policies that are unreasonable, arbitrary, or capricious must be found so by the courts" (Piele, 1979, p. 14).

Faculty unions often seek to infringe on the board's government and management rights and powers by bringing collective bargaining contract clauses to bear. In a number of faculty contracts, boards have negotiated away evaluation procedures and reduced their effectiveness (Andrews, 1985). In moments of weakness or misunderstanding of their responsibilities, boards release their powers to evaluate in formulating the faculty contract.

Piele (1975) points out that no one challenges boards' "authority to develop, adopt, and implement policies, rules, and regulations to govern the school district" (p. 10).

In one case (Irby v. McGowan) a nontenured teacher's contract was not renewed and the teacher sought reinstatement through the court. This was denied by a federal district court that could find no proof of deprivation of liberty or attachment of stigma. The court made a significant statement in terms of boards' rights in evaluation (Piele, 1975): ". . . School authorities should have some right to make subjective evaluations of a work record of a person." The court went on to say: "The court simply cannot, and should not, sit in judgment on, and supervise every remark made concerning the employment or nonemployment of persons in a school system and require that every person not reemployed be entitled to a due process hearing" (p. 196).

Trustees possess final legal authority for their policies in their district. Nason (1982) points out that "only the courts or the legislature can legally challenge a board's decisions" (p. 23). Board action may not suit a faculty member but the board's decision is considered final unless the faculty member intends to go to court. The same is true when it comes to faculty negotiations. Board action becomes the determining factor in the approval process for the final settlement.

In most states, the boards of education are the only bodies that can hire or fire employees, according to Piele (1980). Piele goes on to state that "the board's use of discretion in hiring personnel usually is not qualified or successfully challenged by anyone as long as the letter of the law is not violated" (p. 12).

In secondary schools, boards must hire only qualified teachers. In community colleges, state legislation usually does not spell out faculty qualifications. It is, therefore, imperative that boards have their own district qualifications and competency standards. Illinois Valley Community College has developed a very extensive and well defined *Qualifications and Competency Handbook* for use in guiding its board decisions in hiring, competency development, retrenchments, and firings of faculty. Illinois, like most other states, leaves the question of community college faculty qualifications open to interpretation by the local community college boards.

Board Policies: Defining Standards and Process

The following suggestions of board policies should help to establish expected qualification levels for personnel. The recommendation procedures from appropriate administrators to the president and from the president to the board are included in the first policy.

Hiring Professional Staff. The board should hire a professional staff, educated and prepared in accordance with generally accepted standards and practices for teaching, supervision, and administration in the discipline and subject fields to which they are assigned. These include collegiate study and/or professional experience. As a general rule, graduate work to the Master's degree or beyond in the subjects or fields taught is expected except in such subjects and fields in which college programs are not normally available or in which the work experience and related training is the principal teaching medium. Full-time administrative, faculty, and instructional support positions should be recommended by the president and approved by the board. Full-time college personnel needs should be analyzed by college administrators in various divisions of the college. Recommendation should be made to the president.

While it is common for the board to delegate authority to the chief executive officer for selection of faculty and staff, actual hiring is usually done by the board. Such hirings must advance the goals of the college as they were established and agreed to by the chief executive officer. Should there be a deviation from the established goals because of actions or lack of actions on the part of the hired individual or individuals, the person must be advised of the inconsistency so that they can attempt to remedy the situation.

Recruitment should be preceded by a careful programmatic review including an analysis of personnel needs. Once completed, the president should present the analysis to the governing board for its review, acceptance, and subsequent authorization to recruit needed personnel. The spirit with which a board exercises its right of review is crucial to institutional effectiveness. If the president is unable to get the board to act in a rational, predictable way, then the whole process becomes counterproductive.

No personnel selection procedure can ensure that the right person is always hired, but the chances of making the wrong choice may be greatly reduced by carefully defined procedures. A job description should be prepared that includes both responsibilities and activities of the position to be filled. Criteria should be established by which to measure candidates. The criteria should include the kind of experience, education, or knowledge the candidates must have to perform success-fully. It should be remembered that these criteria are the necessary and absolute minimum requirements and therefore are not negotiable. Additional attributes that the ideal candidate should have should be listed in order of priority. The time frame for filling the vacancy should be announced. Recruitment sources should be appropriate to the position being filled. Of paramount importance is the need for an open search for each and every institutional vacancy to be filled. Institutional safeguards should exist to ensure that openness prevails.

As previously noted, no personnel selection procedure can en-sure that the right person is always hired. Consequently, a board policy requiring continuous evaluation of all personnel should be implemented. There should be a systematic and regular evaluation of all staff, tenured as well as probationary. The following is a suggested policy for such evaluation.

Evaluating Faculty, Assistants to Instruction, and Counselors. It should be board policy to ensure that faculty are evaluated by their supervisors to assure that quality in instruction and professional conduct are maintained. Procedures for such evaluation must be developed and published in the faculty handbook and approved by the board each time the faculty handbook is updated. Persons to be covered by the above mentioned evaluation procedures will be: tenured faculty, nontenured faculty, part-time faculty, counselors, and assistants to instruction. The ultimate decision as to the granting or denying of tenure or the dismissal of a tenured teacher rests with the board. The evaluation procedures provide a means of obtaining information from which to make such a decision.

Establishing Job Descriptions. Employees often find themselves in trouble because they fail to understand the various responsibilities and requirements of their job. Faculty members may feel that, if they teach competently, nothing else matters. This is not the case. There are many other responsibilities and these should be spelled out. Some are outlined in the following job description.

The Full-Time Instructor. The full-time community college instruc-tor is the backbone of the institution and this position is very demanding in terms of preparation and classroom presentation. In addition to the full teaching load as outlined in the faculty contract, instructors are required to perform several other major supportive duties:

1. Serve on advisory committees for occupational programs and for curriculum development,
2. Update and revise curriculum,

3. Serve on college committees as designated by the board of trustees,
4. Put on public performances and displays in such areas as music, speech, theatre, art, and reader's theatre,
5. Participate in cocurricular activities in such areas as athletics, forensics, and field trips,
6. Disseminate information on recruitment of high school students and invitation of potential students for campus visits.

Providing job descriptions can help both administrative and faculty personnel to understand what is expected of a faculty member and can provide a means for evaluation.

Deciding Not to Rehire Nontenured, Full-Time, and Instructional Support Personnel. A decision to not rehire (dismiss) a nontenured faculty member for the ensuing school year or term will be made by the board of trustees. The decision will be made after reviewing the president's recommendation, following an evaluation of the performance and qualifications of such nontenured faculty members. Evaluation procedures to be followed are outlined in the college's faculty handbook. The board will keep the specific reasons for dismissal confidential. These reasons will, however, be issued to the teacher upon request by the teacher. Full-time, nontenured faculty and instructional support personnel who will not be rehired for the next school year or term are to be notified of such a decision no less than sixty days before the end of the school year or term.

The above suggested board policy clearly states the board's responsibility to decide if a nontenured faculty member should not be rehired. (The recommendation is made by the college president to the board.)

Impact of an Effective Evaluation System

There are faculty and administrators who need to be fired. Illinois Valley Community College provides an example of an effective evaluation system in action.

Implemented in 1978, the evaluation system has resulted in the termination, either by dismissal, resignation, or early retirement, of ten long-tenured members of the faculty, nine nontenured, and five administrators. More important, the impact of the system is most apparent in the quality performance of the staff that remains. The staff clearly has been motivated to consciously improve the quality of instruction, enhance professional preparation through attendance at classes or seminars, and perform other professional development activities.

None of the accomplishments were effected without the determined efforts of the board, the president, and the administration, working in accordance with board policies and the established value system.

The initial turmoil that was experienced has given way to organized and supportive efforts to enhance the total quality of the institution. Faculty support is apparent in their willingness to continue their professional development and to be regularly evaluated, and in the increased support for and acceptance of the system. In fact, all members of the college community, including the American Federation of Teachers Local 1810, have become increasingly supportive and take pride in the excellence that pervades the institution.

Knowing the Law

There are many state and federal personnel regulations and laws that have been enacted during the past twenty years. Woodruff (1976) suggests that trustees know these laws to avoid violating basic constitutional rights of employees. He summarizes the following seven rules for trustees:

1. Avoid precipitous action (do not lose your self-control).
2. Make sure you have all the facts. Do not rely on only one side's version of a disputed issue — demand sufficient information before voting.
3. Remember your duty is to the institution you serve, not to any one member of the administration.
4. Follow the rules — the board or college policies and procedures that have been written down.
5. Make an effort to attend every board meeting (by being chronically absent you may incur liability).
6. When in doubt, use your paid professionals; consult your president, chancellor, and counsel.
7. Avoid conflicts of interest by disclosing potential conflict and refusing to debate, discuss, or vote with respect to any matter in which you or your family have an interest.

Summary

The use of the term excellence in education is becoming common. Excellence cannot be perceived in isolated areas of any institution. It is a set of values that must be achieved in all aspects of an institution. It can and should begin with the board of trustees and be reflected by the college personnel. It can be achieved by a board that demands excellence and then sets up a proper personnel management framework.

Boards can and must establish clear and well thought out policies dealing with hiring, evaluating, promoting, and firing of personnel. Legislation in most states clearly designates boards of trustees as the final authority for carrying out the legislation and educational mandates of state educational agencies. Only a court challenge can effect a review of board decisions that are made in accord with their policies.

The exciting challenges of a board, from determining and clarifying those values they believe in for the college to hiring a president, administrative staff, faculty, and support personnel, makes board trusteeship worth pursing.

Prestige for board members will come from good policies, properly administered. Community college students' success at four-year colleges, and in technical jobs, and improvements in community relations give personnel management meaning. The outcomes of a successful personnel management system will more than outweigh *all* other decisions and votes cast by any board members.

Boards must know the law and avoid arbitrary and capricious action in making personnel decisions. They must provide hiring, evaluation, promotion, and dismissal policies and procedures that remove any and all doubt about politically motivated appointments, nepotism, and patronage taking precedence over open search appointments.

There is no amount of financial support that can guarantee excellence in an institution. It requires a dedicated and knowledgeable board and a systematic approach. Patience, time, and fortitude in backing board decisions based on board policies for fostering excellence are necessary parts of the process. Approving a notice to remedy or firing an incompetent faculty member or administrator will test the amount of pressure board members are willing to accept in their commitment to excellence. The community and junior college movement demands and deserves the best efforts that boards of trustees can deliver in personnel management. The students and ultimately society will be the beneficiaries of sound board actions.

References

Andrews, H. A. *Evaluating for Excellence.* Stillwater: New Forums Press, 1985.
Irby vs. *McGowan*, 380 F. Supp. 1024 (S.D. Ala. 1974).
Kauffman, J. F. "Strengthening Chair, CEO Relationships." *AGB Reports*, 1983, *25* (2), 17–21.
McGrath, C. P. "How to Talk to Faculty and Students." *AGB Reports*, 1977, *19* (2), 25–28.

Nason, J. W. "A Sampler from John Nason's *The Nature of Trusteeship.*" *AGB Reports*, 1982, *24* (5), 14–15.

Piele, P. K. (Ed.). *The Yearbook of School Law, 1975.* Topeka, Ka.: National Organization on Legal Problems of Education, 1975.

Piele, P. K. (Ed.). *The Yearbook of School Law, 1980.* Topeka, Ka.: National Organization on Legal Problems of Education, 1980.

Woodruff, B. E. "Trustees Must Know the Law." *AGB Reports*, 1976, *18* (6), 11–18.

Clem R. Jasiek is chair of the Board of Trustees at Illinois Valley Community College, in Oglesby, Illinois.

Alfred Wisgoski is president of Illinois Valley Community College.

Hans A. Andrews is dean of instruction, Illinois Valley Community College.

This chapter lists material abstracted from recent additions to the Educational Resources Information Center (ERIC) system to provide further information on community college governance.

Sources and Information: The Community College Trustee

Diane Zwemer

An earlier New Directions sourcebook, *Enhancing Trustee Effectiveness*, provided a forum for the opinions and concerns of community college trustees in the hopes to "fill the gap that exists in much of the literature on the two-year college" (Dziuba and Meardy, 1976, p. vii). Whereas there is an abundance of literature discussing trusteeship in higher education, there seems to be little focused directly on the two-year college trustee. Since the appearance of that volume, however, literature in this area has steadily increased, particularly during the late 1970s and early 1980s. This review examines the literature on the community college trustee role, the trustee's relationship with the president, trustee orientation, selection, and board characteristics.

The Trustee Role

It is well recorded that the trustee is the governor of the college and the final authority for matters concerning the institution. Trustees do not operate the institution, but establish the policies that are to be executed by the college's administrators (Griffiths, 1979).

But what is the trustees' role in today's educational scene? Many

G. F. Petty (Ed.). *Active Trusteeship for a Changing Era.* New Directions for Community Colleges, no. 51. San Francisco: Jossey-Bass, September 1985.

authors have remarked on the changing environment of higher education and of the community college as having an effect on the trustee's role. Griffiths (1979), Nason (1982) and Potter (1979) all note that trustee authority has eroded over the years due to: (1) the introduction of the GI Bill bringing in new people and new concerns into the higher education arena, (2) the cries for campus democracy during the 1960s, and (3) the declining enrollments and rising costs of the 1970s. At community and junior colleges, trustees struggle with the multiple and often conflicting purposes of the institution (Nason, 1982). Trustees find they are having to meet the demands of both employers and students (Cameron and Needham, 1984). Unless trustees can learn to balance the new and traditional missions of the community college, "the trustee role may well be preempted by legislative dictates" (Richardson, 1981, p. 13). In fact, increased state control rising out of demands for educational accountability has been documented by several authors writing about trusteeship (Cameron and Needham, 1984; Nason, 1982; and Potter, 1979). Other factors facing the community college trustee include divided faculty loyalties and collective bargaining (Nason, 1982; Potter, 1979).

Although trustees are faced with much confusion and uncertainty, Nason calls this a time of opportunity because trustees have the ability to shape the future of all higher education. Several authors have remarked upon the difficult, though potentially optimistic choices the community college trustee must now make. Marsee (1978) recognizes that it is the trustee who needs to create solutions to the problems brought on by a changing society. Ingram (1979) calls for boards to reexamine the community college mission and to stop offering everything to everybody. He also says that boards need to urge greater participation among educational institutions in adopting "sensible cooperative programs in a period of retrenchment" (p. 79). Chapman (1979), like Ingram, feels that the board of trustees is the ideal instigator for interinstitutional cooperation.

The actual duties and responsibilities of the community college trustee are discussed by a number of authors. McLeod (1979) provides a review of the legal responsibilities of local community college governing boards. Trustee duties are discussed by Nason (1982), Potter (1979), and Griffiths (1979); Simpson (1984) writes about the duties of California community college trustees, and Walbourne, (in Phillips and others, 1980) discusses the trustee's role as lobbyist.

The Board-President Relationship

In all trusteeship, perhaps there is nothing so important as the relationship between the board of trustees and the president or chief executive of an institution. One author likens this relationship to a marriage — subject to post-honeymoon blues and early divorce (Ingram, 1979). Another points out the paradoxical nature of the relationship: as the agent of the board the president is accountable directly to them, yet at the same time the board should look to the president for educational leadership (Nason, 1982).

No one disputes that trustees have the responsibility for setting institutional policy while presidents are responsible for establishing the rules and procedures for implementing that policy. However, the line that divides these responsibilities is admittedly not clear (Meardy, 1977; Potter, 1979). The literature stresses that guidelines regarding these responsibilities must be established in order to keep power and authority in the proper place (Meardy, 1977), to maintain institutional reputation and integrity (Ingram, 1979), and to create an atmosphere of mutual trust, respect and confidence (Nason, 1982; Meardy, 1977; Potter, 1979). Much of the literature discussing this relationship concentrates on how to maintain the delicate balance between these two parties.

Hall (1981) writes, "accountability and trust are the two key concepts in the board-presidential relationship" (p. 17). According to Meardy (1977), the president must realize that the board is not just a rubber stamp and must be willing to give the board full disclosure; otherwise, the board may feel enticed to interfere. Ingram (1979) stresses open minds and candidness, while Nason (1982) notes that a board and president cannot play politics with one another. In return, trustees must realize that the president needs support and counsel in order to do an effective job (Meardy, 1977; Marsee [1980]; Ingram, 1979). Furthermore, the board should seek the president's advice when establishing policy (Potter, 1979; Ingram, 1979; Nason, 1982; Hall, 1981).

Most discussions of the board-president relationship include suggestions on how to ensure mutual confidence and respect. Advice directed at the board includes protecting the president from the press and public (Potter, 1979); encouraging the president to have a development program for trustees (Ingram, 1979); refraining from leaking confidential information (Marsee, [1980]); and delegating administrative duties in order to concentrate on policy issues (Nason, 1982). Suggestions for presidents include consistently recognizing the board's policy-making function and being able to know when it is time to move on to a new position (Ingram, 1979). Potter (1979) suggests that each party give the other advance notice of decisions to eliminate surprise and to allow time to react. However, he underscores the importance of respecting the final authority from hence the decision came. Finally,

Seitz (1979) notes that mutually drawn standards of expectations between a new president and a board can not only serve to clear the air and
is also a valuable aid for evaluating the president.

Trustee Orientation

Since one of the primary responsibilities of the trustee is to be
well informed, it is not surprising that almost all trustee literature
touches upon the issue of orientation in some form or other. According to
Griffiths (1979), the vagueness of state law creating boards does not help
the trustee understand how to establish and maintain a college. Moreover, trustees have other demands on their free time and are in need of
assistance when it comes to coping with the rapidly changing educational environment. Most trustees have never attended a community
college and may not understand the special emphasis community colleges give to teaching — as opposed to the research function emphasized
at universities. Gill (1978) notes that, to be effective policy makers,
trustees need to interpret specific community college trends such as
individualized programs, competency-based education, open admis-
sions, articulation programs, and lifelong learning.

According to the literature, effective and informed trustees need
to understand the nature of trusteeship, trends and issues in higher
education, and the characteristics of and local issues facing the college
the trustee is to serve (Nason, 1982; Griffiths, 1979).

Nason (1982) proposes a three-phase orientation program, each
phase focussing on a different aspect. The first phase is at the time of the
invitation, whether by election or appointment, to serve as a trustee.
The president of the college or the board chairman should at that time
review the expectations of a trustee and provide a general orientation on
the institution's character and status. After the trustee has joined the
board, the trustee may be given tours of the college, and may meet with
key personnel to discuss the college. Manuals or handouts on the college
and trusteeship in general are also made available. The third phase
focuses on major problems and issues in higher education that may affect
the college. Special board meetings, workshops, or retreats are suggested for this phase. Orientation programs containing similar elements
have been discussed by Frantzreb (1984), Wygal (1984), and Griffiths,
(1979).

A controversial issue in trustee orientation centers on the role of
the president. Griffiths (1979) notes that there are those who argue that
the president should refrain from any additional opportunity to influ-

ence the board as trustees tend to acquiesce in the face of superior knowledge (see Frederick, 1973). However, this very objection (superior knowledge) is arguably a factor in favor of the president participating in trustee orientation. Frantzreb (1984) places the responsibility for educating trustees directly on the president. If the president does not take the time or effort to instill into trustees knowledge of and respect for the institution, Frantzreb reasons that the president cannot expect trustees to abandon their apathy or to take pride in their duties.

Other authors offer suggestions of programs or practices that have been effective at their college. Wygal (1984), of Florida Junior College at Jacksonville, offers a president's perspective, noting that "trustees need opportunities to fulfill growth and affiliative needs" (p. 49). He encourages membership in the Association of Community College Trustees (ACCT) and schedules special orientation workshops as needed to supply trustees with the information necessary to make decisions. Nicolai (1981), of Yavapai College, Arizona, suggests that an examination of past board meeting minutes may reveal controversial incidents in a board's history that a trustee may wish to know. Caparosa (1984) describes the American Association of Community and Junior College's Building Better Boards Project (BBB). This project grew out of a recognition that board members not only need to understand their fundamental responsibilities but must also have "sophisticated management and leadership skills" (p. 43).

There is a plethora of literature designed to be read by the community college trustee, most of it stemming from the Association of Community College Trustees. One such volume is George Potter's *Trusteeship: Handbook for Community College and Technical Institute Trustees. Second Edition* (1979). Each of its chapters discusses a particular topic related to the trustee role, including trustee responsibilities, the role of the board chair, the relationship between the board and the president, pertinent legal issues, the board's political role, and the board's role in collective bargaining.

The ACCT also produces a journal, *Trustee Quarterly*, whose articles provide information on the nature of trusteeship and trends in education that affect the community college. Articles of particular interest to new trustees have been combined in the publication, *Selected Readings from the Trustee Quarterly* (ACCT, 1982).

Another journal of interest to trustees is the Association of Governing Boards of Universities and Colleges' *AGB Reports*. Published bimonthly, this journal's informative articles are for trustees in all of higher education.

Other orientation literature includes Ingram's *Trustee Workshops*

104

and Retreats, (1978) and *Handbook of College and University Trusteeship* (1980); Scheid (1981), Conger (1981), and Botch and Cartwright [1980].

Trustee Selection

Literature discussing trustee selection centers primarily on the issue of whether trustee appointment or election results in better boards. Nason (1982) notes that, in the public community college, 50 to 60 percent of trustees are elected locally. However, he challenges this method as not necessarily providing the "kind of trustees the community college may need" (p. 64). He feels that elections tend to make trustees adopt party line politics or take a "reform-the-institution" platform that is inconsistent with trustee impartiality. Nason prefers gubernatorial appointment with legislative approval even though appointments may often be made on political, rather than qualitative, grounds. He suggests that a "local screening or nominating committee composed of prominent local citizens" (p. 64) may improve the quality of appointments.

A study comparing the governing effectiveness of appointed and elected boards of trustees was conducted at Wisconsin's vocational-technical schools and community colleges (Ladwig, 1981). The effectiveness of both types of boards were rated by school directors and college presidents in ten areas: affirmative action, board-administrator relations, budget development and approval processes, overseeing the educational program, fiscal accountability to taxpayers, local politics, policy development, qualification and experience of board members, and responsiveness to needs. In general, respondents working under appointed boards felt the boards were extremely effective in the areas of recall of board members, qualifications and experience of board members, and affirmative action—the same areas in which those working under elected boards gave low ratings.

Goddard and Polk (1976), in their review of selection procedures, note that the governor tends to profit from appointment, voters and trustees from election, but there are penalties as well. They conclude that neither way is better for everyone involved.

Bowles's (1979) study on selection criteria for Kansas community college trustees takes a different approach. Instead of assessing trustee effectiveness by method of selection, Bowles sought to identify perceptual differences among community college presidents, faculty and trustees as to what are the appropriate selection criteria for trustees. Among selection criteria noted in the study are: the ability to select, evaluate, and terminate the president; knowledge of purchasing and maintaining facilities; the ability to define the role and mission of the college; the ability to preserve institutional independence; and the ability to create a climate of change.

Board Characteristics

Studies conducted on trustee characteristics tend to support what Nason (1982) refers to as the "standard criticism of governing boards"; that boards are composed of "white, Anglo-Saxon, Protestant, male, well-to-do business and professional men, over fifty in age" (p. 55). Griffiths (1979) notes that most boards in the late 1960s were populated by white, middle-aged, fairly wealthy, corporate executive males. Nason reports on a 1976 national survey of college and university trustees undertaken at the request of the Association of Governing Boards and the American Council on Education that shows similar results: 85 percent of all trustees were then male and 95 percent were white (see Gomber and Atelsek, 1977). In the public two-year college, Nason cites a 1972 survey showing that 85 percent of the trustees are male, 91 percent are white, and 63 percent are over fifty (see Mills, 1972).

How effective are these "alleged monolithic" boards? An effective board, Nason writes, "is more likely to be composed of individuals who bring diverse experiences, talents, and attitudes to the resolution of institutional problems" (p. 57). However, Griffiths (1979) credits Morton Rauh for noting the assumption that diversity improves a board's effectiveness has little or no evidence in support (see Rauh, 1969). Zoglin (1976) writes, "what matters to [trustees'] constituents is how they feel about community college matters, not where they go to church or what income tax bracket they are in" (p. 54). Her review of the relationship between trustee background and performance also notes that there is no conclusive evidence. However, Moore (1973), criticizing community college trustees' background and competence, doubts that a board is a "body of public spirited, selfless, objective, understanding, well informed, apolitical citizens" (p. 1732).

Griffiths, in reviewing studies on trustee characteristics, (including the above mentioned AGB study (1976) and one by the Research Triangle Institute (see Davis and Batchelor, 1974), notes there is an indication that "board composition is changing, but change is slow" (p. 85). Other studies of community college board characteristics include a 1978 study of Arizona community college trustees (Harkins and others, 1978) and a survey of the trustees serving Kansas' nineteen community college districts (Parker and Parker, [1979]).

Regarding women trustees, Bers (1983) notes that very little has been written. In her report on the role of women in community colleges, she concludes her section on trustees by acknowledging that there are "virtually no studies that investigate the relationships between women on boards, advancement of women at their institutions, perceptions and behavior of women trustees regarding their commitment (or lack thereof) to women, or influence of board women on curricula and policies for women students" (p. 27). Smith's (1981) interest in women trustees is to warn them against falling into the trap of spouting one-platform politics. A trustee must serve the whole community, she notes, and "must have a breadth of vision that enables him or her to look beyond the interests of special groups" (p. 56). Smith does recognize the role model function of women trustees, adding, "the trustee who is most effective in advancing the interests of women is the woman who is most effective as a trustee" (p. 58).

An increasing number of teachers and administrators also serve as trustees (Dean, 1981). Advocates of this, writes Zoglin (1976), "feel that those most closely associated with the college should share in the decision-making power and that laymen cannot possess the expertise needed to run today's complex institutions" (p. 64). However, several authors have voiced their concern over the trend. Since boards are expected to serve as a check on the vested interests of internal groups, Dean (1981) suggests that faculty and administrators should not serve on the board of the same college in which they hold a position. Nason (1982) reminds us that faculty prerogatives are only one part of a college's operations. There are even conflicts of interest among faculty, therefore, their inclusion as board members would be "unhealthy and dangerous" (p. 58). Hall (1981) concurs, suggesting as an alternative that "faculty viewpoints can be provided through the president as well as through faculty presentations to the board" (p. 9).

Additional Information

This sampling of ERIC literature has focused primarily on the community college trustee. Additional information on community college trustees or on trusteeship in general may be obtained from manual or computer searches of ERIC's *Resources in Education* or *Current Index to Journals in Education*.

The full text of the references with an ED number may (in most cases) be obtained from the ERIC Document Reproduction Service in Alexandria, Virginia, or viewed on microfiche at over 730 libraries nationwide. References without an ED number must be obtained through regular library channels. For an EDRS order form and/or a list of libraries in your state that have ERIC microfiche collections, please contact the ERIC Clearinghouse for Junior Colleges, 8118 Math-Sciences Building, UCLA, Los Angeles, California, 90024.

References

Association of Community College Trustees (ACCT). *Selected Readings from the Trustee Quarterly: A Special Publication for New Trustees and for Experienced Trustees New to ACCT.* Annandale, Va.: Association of Community College Trustees, 1982. 52 pp. (ED 229 066)

Bers, T. H. "The Promise and Reality of Women in Community Colleges." Paper presented at the Conference of the American Educational Research Association to the Special Interest Group on Women in Education, Tempe, Ariz., November 3–5, 1983. 33 pp. (ED 242 365)

Botch, R., and Cartwright, J. *Better Board Meetings in Less Time.* Moline, Ill.: Black Hawk College, [1980]. 13 pp. (ED 194 149)

Bowles, B. J. "Selection Procedures for Community College Presidents, Trustees and Faculty." Unpublished Ed.D. dissertation, University of Kansas, 1979. (ED 213 439) (Not available from EDRS)

Cameron, D. W., and Needham, R. L. "The Role of Trustees: Policy for Instruction." *Community and Junior College Journal,* 1984, *55* (2), 38–39.

Caparosa, C. "Building Better Boards." *Community and Junior College Journal,* 1984, *55* (2), 42–46.

Chapman, F. C. "But We Haven't Tried Living Together." *AGB Reports,* 1979, *21* (3), 3–5.

Conger, G. P. "Creating Relevant Policies." Paper presented at the Annual Convention of the Association of Community College Trustees, Boston, September 22–26, 1981. 13 pp. (ED 208 906)

Davis, J. A., and Batchelor, S. A. *The Effective College and University Board. A Report of a National Survey of Trustees and Presidents. Final Report.* Durham, N.C.: Research Triangle Institute, 1974. 108 pp. (ED 100 259)

Dean, C. T. "Teachers-Faculty as Trustees: Confrontation or Cooperation?" Paper presented at the Annual Convention of the Association of Community College Trustees, Boston, September 22–26, 1981. 13 pp. (ED 211 144)

Dzuiba, V., and Meardy, W. (Eds.). *Enhancing Trustee Effectiveness.* New Directions for Community Colleges, no. 15. San Francisco: Jossey-Bass, 1976.

Frantzreb, A. C. "Trustee Development Is Everyone's Business." *AGB Reports,* 1984, *26* (6), 20–22.

Frederick, R. W., Jr. *Presidents-Trustees and the Comprehensive Two-Year College.* Albany: New York State Education Department; and Ithaca, N.Y.: State University of New York, Cornell Institute for Research and Development in Occupational Education, 1973. 84 pp. (ED 092 205)

Gill, P. L. *The Trustee and Instructional Programs.* Washington, D.C.: Association of Community College Trustees, 1978. 22 pp. (ED 156 303)

Goddard, J. M., and Polk, C. H. "Community College Trustees: Elect or Appoint?" *AGB Report,* 1976, *18* (3), 37–40.

Gomber, I., and Atelsek, F. *Composition of College and University Governing Boards. Higher Education Panel Report Number 35.* Washington, D.C.: American Council on Education, 1977. 28 pp. (ED 144 514)

Griffiths, A. A. (Ed.). *Appendices to Excellence and the Open Order: An Essential Partnership. A Report of the Commission to Study the Mission, Financing, and Governance of the County Colleges, State of New Jersey. Volume Two.* Trenton: New Jersey State Board of Higher Education, 1979. 108 pp. (ED 168 649)

Hall, R. A. *Challenge and Opportunity: The Board of Trustees, the President, and Their Relationship in Community College Governance.* Annandale, Va.: Association of Community College Trustees, 1981. 29 pp. (ED 201 362)

Harkins, C. L., and others. *A Study of District Governing Boards.* Phoenix: Arizona State Board of Directors for Junior Colleges, 1978. 57 pp. (ED 154 869)

Ingram, R. T. *Trustee Workshops and Retreats.* Washington, D.C.: Association of Governing Boards of Universities and College, 1978. 12 pp. (ED 196 355)

Ingram, R. T. "The Marriage of Presidents and Boards." In R. E. Lahti (Ed.), *Managing a New Era.* New Directions for Community Colleges, no. 28. San Francisco: Jossey-Bass, 1979.

Ingram, R. T., and others. *Handbook of College and University Trusteeship.* San Francisco: Jossey-Bass, 1980.

Ladwig, D. "Comparison of Governance Effectiveness of Appointed and Elected Boards of Education/Trustees." Unpublished doctoral dissertation, Nova University, 1981. 49 pp. (ED 214 559)

McLeod, M. W. *Patterns of Responsibility: Statutory Requirements of Community College Local Boards of Trustees.* Annandale, Va.: Association of Community College Trustees, 1979. 43 pp. (ED 201 363)

Marsee, S. E. *The Community in Community College.* Torrance, Calif.: El Camino College, 1978. 22 pp. (ED 151 053)

Marsee, S. E. *The President's Relationship to the Board.* Unpublished paper, [1980]. 8 pp. (ED 186 072)

Meardy, W. H. "Working Relationship Between Presidents and Trustees." In *Proceedings [of the] Annual Governor's Workshop for Community College Trustees (1st, Tallahassee, Florida, August 5–6, 1977).* Tallahassee: Florida State Dept. of Education, Division of Community Colleges, 1977. 41 pp. (ED 151 060)

Mills, P. K. "Community College Trustees: A Survey." In *The Two Year College Trustee: National Issues and Perspectives.* Washington, D.C.: Association of Governing Boards of Universities and Colleges, 1972. 40 pp. (ED 073 757)

Moore, W., Jr. "The Community College Board of Trustees: A Question of Competency." *Journal of Higher Education,* 1973, *44* (3), 171–190.

Nason, J. W. *The Nature of Trusteeship: The Role and Responsibilities of College and University Boards.* Washington, D.C.: Association of Governing Boards of Universities and Colleges, 1982. 127 pp. (ED 226 648; available in microfiche only)

Nicolai, M. C. "I Became a Trustee: Now What?" Paper presented at the 1981 Pacific Region Seminar of the Association of Community College Trustees, "Blazing New Trails in the 80s," Portland, June 25–27, 1981. 9 pp. (ED 205 248)

Parker, P., and Parker, P. W. *Decade One+Four: Profile of the Kansas Trustee.* Pittsburg: Kansas State College, [1979]. 27 pp. (ED 181 991)

Phillips, H. E. and others. "Lobbying State Legislatures." Transcript of a presentation given at the Annual Conference of the American Association of Community and Junior Colleges, San Francisco, Calif., March 30-April 2, 1980. 25 pp. (ED 191 533)

Potter, G. E. *Trusteeship: Handbook for Community College and Technical Institute Trustees.* (2nd Ed.) Annandale, Va.: Association of Community College Trustees, 1979. 180 pp. (ED 201 368; available in microfiche only)

Rauh, M. A. *The Trusteeship of Colleges and Universities.* New York: McGraw Hill, 1969.

Richardson, R. C., Jr. "Trustees and Missions of Arizona Community Colleges." Paper presented to the Arizona Association of Local Governing Boards, September 18, 1981. 15 pp. (ED 211 150)

Scheid, C. "Our Board Was Caught Short." *AGB Reports*, 1981, *23* (6), 31–33.

Seitz, J. E. "Evaluating Your President Objectively: A Message to Trustees." Paper presented at the National Meeting of the Association of Community College Trustees, Detroit, Mich. 1979. 17 pp. (ED 191 524)

Simpson, R. H. *The Neglected Branch: California Community Colleges.* Sacramento: California State Legislature, Senate Office Research, 1984. 86 pp. (ED 243 506)

Smith, J. A. "A View from the Board of Trustees." In J. S. Eaton (Ed.), *Women in Community Colleges.* New Directions for Community Colleges, no. 34. San Francisco: Jossey-Bass, 1981. (ED 203 929)

Wygal, B. R. "Agenda for Excellence: Leadership for the Board." In J. E. Roueche and G. A. Baker III (Eds.), *Community College Leadership for the '80s.* AACJC Leadership Bookshelf Series, No. 1. Washington, D.C.: American Association of Community and Junior Colleges, 1984. 76 pp. (ED 251 162; available in michofiche only)

Zoglin, M. L. *Power and Politics in the Community College.* Palm Springs, Calif.: ETC Publications, 1976. 166 pp. (ED 138 322) (Not Available from EDRS)

Diane Zwemer is user services librarian at the ERIC Clearinghouse for Junior Colleges, University of California, Los Angeles.

Index

111